Being Israeli After the Destruction of Gaza

Being Israeli After the Destruction of Gaza
By Ariel Beery

The interviews in this book have been edited for length and clarity. Some identifying details have been changed at the request of participants.

First published on Yom Ha'atzmaut, 5786 (2026)

Prophecy Press, Zichron Yaakov
seekprophecy.com

ISBN: 9798995789611

For our children.

May you inherit an Israel worthy of you.

חזק ואמץ.

Table of Contents

A Note on the Interviews

The conversations in this book took place between January and March, 2026. Each was conducted by video call and recorded with the knowledge and consent of the participant. Transcripts were edited for length and clarity; in some cases, a subject's responses to different questions have been reorganized to improve the flow of the written account, while preserving the substance and spirit of what was said.

Each participant was given the opportunity to review their chapter prior to publication and to request factual corrections. None of the participants was paid. None was given editorial control over the framing, context, or conclusions drawn from the conversation.

The people interviewed for this book were not selected to represent a statistical cross-section of Israeli Jewish society. They were selected because they represent a position I believe has been underrepresented in the international media: liberal democratic Israelis who are Zionists, who opposed the Netanyahu government's judicial overreach and its conduct of the war in Gaza, and who have nonetheless not abandoned the project.

Readers looking for voices from the Netanyahu-supporting Israeli right, the ultra-Orthodox community, or non-Jewish Israeli society will need to look elsewhere, and I hope they do so to broaden their understanding of Israeli society.

Introduction

"Zionism's hard gift to the Jews," writes Yossi Klein Halevi in *At the Entrance to the Garden of Eden*, "was to force us to assume our place among the morally ambiguous nations, pry us from the comfortable self-image of a helpless people to accept responsibility for our fate."

I've returned to those words again and again since October 7th, 2023: when thinking about the Hamas attacks that morning; when remembering the murder of civilians in their homes, the kidnapping of families from their beds; when thinking about the collapse of the assumption that whatever dangers came, the state would ultimately protect us.

I returned to Yossi's words as the war in Gaza unfolded. When entire neighborhoods were flattened. When whole families were killed. I found the images of entire populations made homeless impossible to ignore. Many Israelis, including myself, believed the war could have been fought differently, and perhaps ended sooner. Yet the reality we faced was one in which power served the politics of a government we did not trust and a leader we did not support.

Like many Israelis, I had spent the year before the attacks in the streets. In reaction to the government's campaign to dismantle the judiciary and tighten its grip on the state, hundreds of thousands of us protested the government every

Saturday night, week after week, for months. Our fight was to ensure Israel remains a liberal democracy. The symbol of the protest was the Israeli Flag, leading to a cognitive dissonance of sorts for some abroad, a tension between our core identity and the way our state was increasingly being identified.

Then came the war. For many of us in the democracy movement, liberals and progressives alike, the way the government conducted the war in Gaza further deepened our distrust, expanding the gap between our commitment to our national project and our identification with that same government.

Abroad, however, that distinction was not acknowledged. A dissonance developed: many of the people we had assumed would be our allies in opposing Netanyahu's government and rescuing the liberal, democratic Israel from its grips, turned on us – treating all Israelis as if we were one and the same with the government we opposed.

That dissonance was reflected in the wave of posts and essays and books that used the destruction of Gaza to argue against Zionism itself. Some were written by people who no doubt wish me and the Jewish People harm. Those I could set aside. Others I couldn't, because they were written by people I had previously disagreed with but respected: Peter Beinart, Shaul Magid, Avraham (Avrum) Burg. Their central claim, often either printed in the New York Times or other equivalently popular and powerful media, is that the destruction of Gaza proved Zionism was destined for failure, that genocide was a feature of Zionism and not a bug. Reading those hit me hard. Not because I found their cases convincing, but because I found myself struggling to explain why I didn't. My objection was instinctual, emotional, reflexive. I was at a loss for words when seeking to describe Zionism as a morally justifiable idea in light of the morally ambiguous reality it had created. And I felt that if I was feeling so, there must be others who felt, like me, that there was something deeply wrong with these critiques. Others searching for words to describe their intuition.

So I did what I do when I do not yet have the words to explain to myself how I feel: I spoke with others. Specifically, I sought out people who were, like me, committed to liberal democracy in Israel. People who believe that every person was created in the image of the Eternal, and has equal value. People who are Zionists, even today, especially today, and who in the same breath as defending the justice of the State's existence do not hesitate to criticize and protest and denounce the government that failed to prevent October 7th and then directed Israel's longest and bloodiest war.

I asked them: how does it feel to be Israeli after the destruction of Gaza?

This book is my attempt to share the words I heard. To share their reflections on the past three years alongside their visions for the future.

Because while I entered those conversations with trepidation – fearing I might find my friends demoralized, broken, questioning – what I found was something else entirely: resolve.

The people I spoke with acknowledged the same painful truths: that October 7th represented a catastrophic failure of the Israeli state, that the war that followed caused immense suffering to Palestinians in Gaza, that Israel's political leadership had acted irresponsibly in the years leading up to this moment. But none of them agreed with Beinart, with Burg, with Magid, with the dozens of other platformed anti-Zionist voices. None of them concluded that the answer was to abandon the project. Each of them carried the weight of a morally ambiguous reality in which we live, and decided to stay with the complexity and bear the responsibility rather than to resolve it by giving up sovereignty to return to a state of powerlessness.

The people I spoke with are by no means representative of the whole of the political spectrum, yet each represents a significant enough portion of our civilization to be worth listening to. They all began with their personal story of October 7th, and each willingly and openly grappled with the war since, its consequences, and its implications. At times I did not share their opinion. Yet it was through reviewing my own experience of the attacks and the war through their stories that I came to better understand myself, my relationship to my Israeli identity, and my fellow Israelis. I hope you feel similarly: that by reading about their experiences you too will find, if not clarity, then at least the words to describe how you feel about Israel given all that has happened since that cursed day.

Readers may notice that the voices I decided to include in this book are all insider-outsiders, Israelis who were either born abroad or lived abroad, who worked within Israeli civil society while being constantly conscious of Israel's standing in the world. Readers may also notice that I chose not to include individuals who served in Gaza because I did not want to ask any individual to justify their actions. Each person interviewed had loved ones or knew people they loved who served. I found that keeping one step removed from the fighting was best suited for a more open conversation.

Also, it is important for me to explain why I decided not to include voices of non-Jewish Israelis despite their growing centrality in Israeli society. I did so because I did not believe I could, at this time, accurately and faithfully communicate their experiences since October 7th, or their evolving relationship with the state and the Zionist movement. I am aware that this exclusion has a cost, and that the Jewish nature of the state matters deeply to its non-Jewish citizens. This book's silence on their experience is a limitation. I hope others will take up the cause to express their voices with the seriousness and dignity they deserve as Israelis with a stake in the future of the state.

I began this book immediately after the announcement of the second phase of the ceasefire between Gaza and Israel in January 2026, and the return of the living hostages. The book was edited and revised during Israel and America's forty day war with Iran, and finished after a two week ceasefire was declared. It is impossible for me to know in which reality you will be reading this, yet I believe the ideas conveyed by the people interviewed for this book will remain relevant. I am also sure that they – alongside their peers and neighbors – will not give up hope, will not forfeit their responsibility, for the future of Israel, or for the future of Gaza.

I hope this book will help readers better understand what the not-so-silent majority of Israelis actually think – those fighting for a more liberal, more democratic future for Israel, who return to the streets whenever there is a pause in the bombardment of our civilian centers. The ones who are committed to building a better future, the ones who recognize the complexity of the world we live in. The ones willing to grapple with the contradictions, sleeves rolled up, hands blistered from doing the work of rebuilding that which was broken. I came away inspired from these conversations, and I hope to convey that inspiration to you in the pages to come.

Meredith Mishkin Rothbart

"Gary, I don't think I can be a peacebuilder."

Meredith Mishkin Rothbart texted these words to Gary Mason in the days after October 7th, after he checked in to see how she was doing. Gary is a Methodist minister from Northern Ireland who spent decades mediating between paramilitaries during the Troubles, one of the people credited for the tough, backbreaking work of building peace behind the scenes. Gary had sat across from men who had ordered killings and helped them find their way toward peace. The IRA literally put down their guns in his church. He has since become one of the world's most respected figures in conflict resolution. When the violence in Israel began, he reached out to Meredith. And she felt, at the moment, that she was disappointing him.

Meredith got to know Gary over the years of building Amal-Tikva, an organization she co-founded with Basheer Abu Baker, a Palestinian citizen of Israel. Together they had created something rare: a peacebuilding infrastructure that worked across the divide. Their programs brought Jews and Palestinians together for sustained dialogue, for professional development, creating deep and abiding relationships between leaders in both people's civil societies. Their leadership initiative has trained over three hundred peacebuilders, creating a network of people committed to coexistence across the region and the world. They had channeled more than a million dollars in new funding to Israeli and Palestinian NGOs doing similar work, strengthening a field that often struggled for resources and recognition. Meredith was the CEO. Basheer was the CFO. The organization's name means "hope" in both Arabic and Hebrew, a linguistic bridge of equal grounding in both cultures.

And now Meredith couldn't imagine continuing.

"I don't know when I'm going to be able to," she told Mason.

"Give yourself two weeks," he replied. "The world will look really different in two weeks."

She was not alone. In the weeks after October 7th, I heard versions of this same confession from peacebuilders across Israel, people who had devoted their careers to the belief that coexistence was possible, that human-to-human relationships could outlast political failure. Many lived on or worked with the people on the kibbutzim attacked by Hamas. Some of these peacebuilders had spent decades building dialogue programs, youth exchanges, shared business ventures. They had staked their personal and professional lives on the proposition that Israelis and Palestinians could live in coexistence, that we had a future in this region that could be marked by collaboration and not killing.

For a time, I lived among them. When I made aliyah (moved to Israel) in 1998, I did so to a kibbutz called Kerem

Shalom, whose fields are literally pressed up against the border with Gaza's Khan Younis. It was there that I met Yael Agmon.

Yael was a long-time peace activist and resident of the kibbutz approximately my parents' age, who had made Kerem Shalom her home since the glory days of the 1970s when the kibbutz was notorious for its radical activism and sexual freedom. By the time I made it to the Kerem Shalom, the kibbutz had fallen apart and had reconstituted. Parts of the kibbutz were left as a time capsule, little changed from the days when young women and men would wake up at five in the morning to work the fields. Weeds grew in between the cracks in their abandoned workshops, farm equipment stood in place, having seen better days. I fell in love with the land, with how the grass kissed the dunes come rain, the low trees and cool mornings and scorching noons. I immersed myself into the history of the kibbutz and joined in the fulfillment of its mission.

Those were the heady days of the Oslo Peace Process, years before Yasser Arafat would order the bloody attacks that catalyzed the Second Intifada, when many felt that peace was just around the corner. Inspired by Yael, Yatir Sade and Chen Arnon from my Garin (our movement cohort) organized a trip to Gaza, to build relations with local Gazans and advance the people-to-people ties we believed would help the Oslo process transition from an agreement between elites to a cultural reality between both peoples. I joined them in founding what we came to call the *First of May Project*, an initiative intended to build an alliance between socialist movements on both sides of the border dedicated to improving the lives and livelihoods of the agricultural and industrial workers who were the beating heart of the region's economy. It was through that work that I met many of the peace activists who lived then in the region, who had dedicated their lives to advancing coexistence one day at a time.

At first, the *First of May* was a success. We organized a conference for over a hundred activists, a third from Gaza, a third from Israel, and a third from Ramallah. We organized a tour of Gaza. We visited the newly opened airport, we ate hummus and drank thick coffee at the headquarters of the Palestinian navy, and we observed the disparity between the beachside villas of Gazan elite and the poor stacked up against their walls. We organized a tour of Tel Aviv, picking up Gazans at the Erez Crossing and taking them to meet with leaders in the arts, in activism. We ate together, traveled together, planned a better future together.

Arafat's Second Intifada shattered the momentum for the *First of May*, as it did most peace initiatives of that time, scattering those young leaders across their societies and across the world. It would take decades for new programs to emerge and rededicate themselves to Yael's mission to build ties between Israel and Gaza. Many of those leaders continued to live, like Yael, on the kibbutzim surrounding the Gaza Strip. Some of those leaders, like Vivian Silver, were brutally dragged from their homes October 7th or murdered on that terrible day. Some survived. And the massacre shattered something fundamental in almost all of them.

I know it did in me too, for a while. If Hamas could do this to the very people who had devoted their lives to improving the lives of Gazans, if the people you had sat across from in dialogue could celebrate the slaughter of your loved ones, then what had all the work been for? What had any of it meant? The question hung over every peacebuilder I spoke with in those first weeks. Some would find their way back to the work. Others would not.

Which is why I wanted to speak with Meredith, one of Israel's leading lights on coexistence. I've known Meredith since 2006, when she was a twenty-year-old undergraduate at the University of Pittsburgh, founding STAND: Students Taking Action Now: Darfur. I was introduced to her by Aaron Weil, the Hillel Director at Pittsburgh, a friend I had gotten to know during my military service in Israel.

At first she joined me and other volunteers at PresenTense Magazine as a writer and copyeditor. Soon thereafter she pitched me on a Middle East Peace House – a place where Arabs, Palestinians, and Jews would live under one roof – for a fellowship at the first PresenTense Institute for Creative Zionism in Jerusalem, an accelerator for mission-driven innovation I cofounded with Aharon Horwitz in 2007. The idea seemed impossibly idealistic, even then. I loved it.

I've followed Meredith's professional journey ever since. To me she represents the Jewish approach to coexistence at its most sincere: deeply religiously attuned, deeply committed to human dignity, grounded in the belief that all peoples between the River and the Sea deserve self-determination, unwavering in its confidence that a Jewish state is both historically just and necessary for Jewish survival – even if it fails to protect Jews or harms others at times.

When I reached out to Meredith I had a single question: how has the destruction of Gaza affected your thinking about Israel? But to get there, we had to start at the beginning: how she remembered Israel on October 6, before the attacks, before the bloodshed and the years of war.

"I remember that night really clearly. It was euphoric," she immediately answered. It had been a rough week for her, but Friday night at shul (synagogue) was something else entirely.

"Friday night at shul was just like a level of feeling close and connected to God and my community and my family, my kids and husband. It literally felt like everything had been building towards this moment. And everyone felt that. There was just this vibe at *shul*. Everyone was really looking forward to the next day."

This is something people who do not know Meredith sometimes miss: she is deeply religious. Her commitment to coexistence is not liberalism dressed in Israeli clothing. It grows from her deep faith, from a belief that redemption will come if we bring it, that the Jewish people have a role to play, and that role includes ethical responsibility toward the people who share this land. "God didn't put us here with another people by accident. He knew exactly what he was doing. This is our big test."

That Friday night, surrounded by her community, Meredith felt that her life made sense. She and her husband Zack had built a home in Jerusalem, raised four wonderful children. She ran a coexistence organization with a Palestinian partner. Everything she had worked for was taking shape.

Then she went to sleep. And in the morning, the world she knew came apart.

"We were up really late, so we let everybody sleep in. I don't remember what time the sirens started in Jerusalem, but me and the kids were in pajamas. My husband was getting changed. I heard the siren and I yelled, 'Zacky!' And he yelled, 'Go!' And I just grabbed the kids and ran down four flights of stairs to the miklat (bomb shelter)."

They waited in the bomb shelter with their neighbors. When they came back up, she told the kids not to worry.

"I said, 'Don't worry, there's never more than one.' I told them to get dressed just in case and we'll get ready to go to shul, but it's fine."

Then there was another siren. And another. And the vibe in the building shifted.

"There's a woman from our building who was in Keva (professional army service). She pulled Zack aside. She knew he was in the reserves with a high security clearance. She told him what was happening. He offered her our car to get to her base."

The woman's response stayed with Meredith.

"She said, 'You're going to need it.'"

They decided to go to shul anyway, since it is based out of a school with a big bomb shelter. Sirens kept coming. Men turned on their phones, breaking Shabbat to check rumors about who had been called up. Meredith sat on the floor of the shelter nursing her nine-month-old during the Torah reading.

"I just kept thinking, 'This war will have a name.' That was like my mantra. I've been through the wars in 2012, 2014, 2021. I didn't have any reason that morning to think this was any different."

After shul, they went back home to prepare lunch. Her parents were too scared to leave their house where they have a safe room, so she decided to bring the food to them.

"So much of my emotional energy that morning was thinking about the brisket. If my parents aren't going to come, they're not going to have any food. But if we bring the brisket to them, it's not going to be hot."

As she was packing up the food, a siren went off.

"I turned and spilled all the juice of the brisket all over my kitchen floor. I just left it, grabbed the kids, and ran to my parents' place. We left the brisket juice on the floor."

Her father had turned on his iPad. He was watching the news.

"He was like, 'It's over. We're all gonna die. There's not gonna be Israel. They're everywhere. Hamas took over the country.' I took him into his bedroom and I was like, stop. My kids are coming. We're going to have a normal Shabbat. You can keep your crazy in your room."

Around one in the afternoon, Zack got called up to join his reserve unit.

"We tried to act calm. At first we didn't tell the kids he was leaving. But later when it was time to say goodbye, I felt like I wasn't ever going to see him again."

Zack had always told her what a wartime call-up would mean.

"He said if he ever got called during a war, it was Armageddon. And so the fact that he was being called meant it was Armageddon. He only packed for three days because we hadn't done laundry. I was sure I was going to be a single mom and maybe I was even going to have to move back to America."

After Shabbat ended, she finally opened her phone.

"One of my friend's sons was already killed. And that just felt like, okay, here it goes."

Her team immediately understood the enormity of the hour. "Basheer called me and I said, 'Are you okay?' He said, 'Yeah, are you?' I said, 'No.' He said, 'I'm going to the supermarket. Do you need anything? I'm assuming Zack's in the army.' And I said, 'I'm staying at my parents.' And he was like, 'Good.' I said, 'Be careful. People are going to be really scared.' He said, 'I'll be careful.'" Then her head of operations called her. "We're going to have to change our whole curriculum," she said. Meredith responded: "I'm really glad that you are thinking about our curriculum right now. I am not there."

Basheer checked in with her every day, until Meredith was ready to come back to work. On the other hand, her friends in the space were not as fortunate. A Jewish colleague told her a few weeks into the war, "No one held space for me. No one on the Palestinian side reached out to say, 'Are you okay?' Not one person."

She does not blame them. A Palestinian who expresses public sympathy for Jews risks social destruction: lost business, severed family ties, community exile. "I understand the consequences they face. If they say anything publicly that sounds like sympathy for Jews, their whole community might turn on them. I've seen it happen. But it doesn't make the silence less painful. One of my younger staff said in the first few weeks of the war, 'for us Palestinians, it's like October 7th every day.' That really stuck with me."

Even among Meredith's inner circle there were tensions. "I was single-parenting four kids while running the organization. I didn't even have time to read the news. And even with Basheer, who we had been literally together every day for eight years. It was the first time that we felt like there was a wall between us. We had an argument one day about the differences between how Israeli and Palestinian media were reporting what happened. I couldn't hold it and couldn't look at him. We didn't speak for a few days."

The wall metaphor especially stood out to me when she described it, because when I think Meredith, I think bridges. I think about the years she spent teaching others to see each other's pain, believing that each of us is a reflection of the divine deserving of care, support, acknowledgement. The pain, the anguish she felt when seeing the walls come up was and remains visceral to me. It was the reason she told Gary Mason she couldn't continue, and why she was so relieved he said to take a bit of time.

"Taking two weeks meant I didn't have to decide today. It meant I could grieve and be scared in the moment, and figure out my role once things calmed down."

But in the third week she decided to return to the office. The office itself had undergone a renovation, and all the furniture had been delivered in boxes. Flat-pack IKEA furniture for a 250 square-meter office with seven rooms.

"We didn't really know how to interact with each other. We didn't really know what to talk about. We were all kind of scared to open the conversation. So we said we'll spend the first three days just building all the furniture together and ordering lunch. And that was it."

And as people do, as they built furniture they started talking.

"People could start to talk while building furniture because you're not making eye contact. You're kind of busy." If emotions ran hot, she told me, they could always take a break by going to a different room, "fix a different chair, help each other. We ordered big lunches every day. And that kind of just got us back into functioning together."

She told her staff they weren't having formal dialogue circles.

"We're not sitting in a circle and having dialogue while it's still happening. We're just going to be together. Be open."

One of the first times Zack came home on leave, as the war was still raging in its earliest stages, he came in the middle of the day. It was pouring rain. He needed the car and didn't have keys to the house, so he came to the office in uniform, with a gun and a big bag.

"I said, call me when you're downstairs. I'll come out and give you the keys. I don't want you coming into my office" with his gun and uniform, given the Palestinian teammates who were there and the feelings that seeing him could elicit.

That bothered him. "He was like, 'I'm protecting them too.' I was like, 'They don't see it that way.' Here he is, already weeks in the army, and I won't even let him in my office. It was complicated and I felt really torn. I went with my gut."

Meredith was in a meeting with Basheer when Zack arrived. She told Basheer she needed to run down and give Zack the keys.

"And Basheer was like, 'I'm going to come down with you.' He walked out with me and shook Zack's hand and gave him a hug and said, 'Thank you for protecting us.'"

She let the weight of that moment sit.

"Basheer's family is from the north. Zack was literally protecting his family. That was really intense. Here's my Palestinian co-director, who cannot publicly acknowledge what Hamas did, hugging my husband in the rain and thanking him for his service. That's the complexity. That's what I live inside of every day."

And with that, I asked about what Israel did in the months, in the years, following Hamas' brutal attacks on October 7th, 2023. How she felt about the idea of Israel throughout this period, how she as a humanist (albeit from a religious starting point) felt about the use of unbridled power and the pain it can cause to people she knew so well.

"Between my brother, my husband, and having served myself, I know we make mistakes. I know we're not perfect. But I trust that the leadership of our military is trying to do its best. The government, on the other hand...I don't trust Bibi to make decisions from a good place. I don't trust our government right now and that makes trusting the army complicated, because they ultimately have to answer to the government."

She took a deep breath.

"I am broken by what we had to do in Gaza. But I don't know if there was another way. I am not an expert in military strategy. I think October 7th was our fault in many ways. And once it happened, every option was terrible."

I asked whether she still believes the work of coexistence makes sense after everything that happened. Whether she still believes peace is possible given everything that happened between our two peoples.

"We are not going to end the war," she told her colleagues early on. "If you need to go out in the streets because you need to be focused on getting the hostages out or ending the war, I understand that. That is not Amal-Tikva. That is not our role. Our role is to make sure that we are not in this place in twenty years, thirty years. We are building a slow, sustainable, changed reality. We're making sure October 7th doesn't happen again. We're not dealing with the fallout of it."

And that is when I heard her say what I have found missing from so many critiques of Zionism from the liberal or progressive side abroad, so many theoretical conversations about whether the Jews, or Israel, can ever 'rebound' from the war: "Everything we're doing now is just practice. It's going to be bigger and bigger, higher and higher stakes. It's not like we get to some point and it's 'peace now' and it's over. It's always going to be part of the work. But you get through a generation of people who have lived in a reality where we're not constantly at war and constantly killing each other, it will already feel more stable."

But does Jewish sovereignty matter to you? I pressed, since I know many of her peers abroad (and some in Israel) have come to argue that the Jewish nature of the State is at the root of the problem. And since I knew that Meredith, as a person of deep faith in the messianic age, may prioritize Jewish life on the land over Jewish control of it.

"I felt that way maybe ten years ago," she said. "I remember sitting in the PresenTense Institute with Jitzhak Rosenbloom being like, 'Oh my gosh, we're more left-wing than the left wing because we don't even care [about the modern State].' But now...I'm not willing to give up sovereignty. That's from a place of keeping us safe. I don't trust anybody else at the end of the day, in the long term, to look out for our well-being."

While some may believe that the Jews are better off seeking to work within universalist political frameworks where they will not be the majority, where they will depend on the cooperation of others for power, Meredith does not. She believes both peoples can fulfill their national and religious aspirations here, but she also believes it would be naive to imagine that Jews can place their lives in the hands of others.

"I don't expect the Palestinians I work with to be anything other than Muslims who, at the end of the day, might want us to leave. But the people who work with me, as much as they would like me to leave and get out of their face and even if they believe we should never have come here to begin with, they're choosing peaceful means to try to fix it and come to a new reality. Just like I am."

When I asked about Basheer, her voice shifted.

"Basheer has limits to what he can say, what he can do, who he can be publicly. I understand that. But understanding it doesn't make it easier."

Meredith's story is, in some ways, the story of liberal and progressive Zionism after October 7th, after the destruction of

Gaza. Perhaps a bit more religiously infused, definitely more politically and socially engaged than most Jews and Arabs, yet a reflection of the original Zionist vision: a Jewish home in the Land of Israel at peace with the peoples of the region. Meredith's story, to me, reflects the hope that preceded this terrible war. The rupture that followed. The slow, painful work of deciding what to do now.

She has not abandoned the work. She has not abandoned her relationship with Palestinian society. She has not forgotten the pain, does not believe this was the last war, yet she keeps on building the infrastructure to enable our two peoples to live side by side.

I wanted to begin this book with Meredith because her story raises the questions I believe we need to ask ourselves after the fighting has ceased, now that the dust is settling in Gaza and we can assess the human cost of the past few years. I believe hers to be a much more embodied exploration of what was, what is, and what should be than the critics from afar who are calling on the Jewish People to abandon the Zionist idea. While the others I spoke with were perhaps less religious than Meredith, perhaps less committed to peacebuilding on a daily basis, they shared her practicality, her groundedness. And I believe these are the voices the world needs to hear when thinking about the future of Israel, the future of Palestine, the future of being Jewish.

Daniel Gordis

"When I look at those moonscapes," Rabbi Dr. Daniel ("Danny") Gordis told me, "my overwhelming reaction is one of just like, I can't speak. Not guilt, not 'we shouldn't have done it'. I just can't speak."

Danny had difficulty describing to me how he feels when he sees the images from Gaza: the flattened neighborhoods, the rubble that stretches to the horizon. "It looks like Dresden. It looks like Hiroshima."

Danny has spent his career helping American Jews understand Israel, through his email listserv, through books, through his podcast, through decades of public writing, through a career of service. He made aliyah in 1998 – the same year I did for the first time – and I got to know over the years of his hosting PresenTense fellows in his office to talk about the world of Jewish education and public service. I remember thinking how refreshing it was to meet someone more religious than I am, more right-wing than I am, with whom I shared many fundamental values. And that is why I wanted to hear what he thought about the destruction of Gaza.

"I hear multiple voices in my head," he told me. "One of those voices, and I'm not necessarily proud of it, but I'm going to be super honest with you...One of those voices is: don't screw with the Jews anymore. You can't do that. You can't come across our border, steal our children, murder our children, set them on fire, rape people, take them into Gaza, and think we're going to fire some missiles back at you. No, those days are over. That's the difference between Gaza and Kishinev," he reflects, recalling the massacre of Jews in 1903 immortalized by Chayim Nahman Bialik's *In the City of Slaughter*, a poem that held a mirror to the powerlessness of the shtetl Jew. "In Kishinev, it was only over when *they* said it was over. In the Otef," the communities on the border of Gaza, "it was over when *we* decided it was over."

That reference hit me hard. Because it rang true. Kishinev, as a paradigmatic pogrom representing the experience of generations of Jews living after the Roman exile, is a much better reference to the massacres of October 7th than, in my opinion, the Holocaust.

"This is the first time in my life," he told me, "that I think I've ever really understood what it means to be a Jew."

To understand what Danny means, I think it is worth going back to the year before October 7th. The year of the Netanyahu government's campaign for judicial reform, the year of mass protests, the year the country nearly tore itself apart. "2023 was a horrible year," he said. "Minister of Justice Yariv Levin rolled out the judicial reform at the very beginning of January, after Bibi [Prime Minister Benjamin Netanyahu] explicitly promised that it wasn't part of their agenda."

Danny had watched the crisis unfold with a historian's eye. He understood why different groups supported weakening the judiciary: the Haredim worried about draft exemptions, the settlers hoped the Supreme Court would stop blocking annexation, the Mizrahim felt the judiciary had become an Ashkenazi elite replicating itself. He brought people onto his podcast from across the spectrum: Moshe Koppel, the intellectual architect of the reform; Yaniv Roznai, who warned it would end Israeli democracy; Netta Barak-Corren, who tried to chart a middle path. I listened to those interviews, and was impressed by how Danny could always keep his cool while I nearly boiled over at times.

"I wanted to check in with people who are much smarter than me, who were all over the map, to hear from them: what do you really think is going on?"

What he found was a country divided on an existential basis: a country with distinct communities who had nearly contradictory views of what Israel should be and how it should be governed. Each community was certain that justice was on its side, willing to risk it all to ensure Israel become or remain the State they understood it to be. The reservists who said they wouldn't serve if democracy was dismantled. The protesters who blocked highways in rage. The government that drove the legislation at an accelerated clip without any regard for those who felt the reform deserved more consideration and public debate. Government supporters who attacked protesting citizens and ripped up their signs.

Despite the chaos, the crisis, his concern for the tearing of the social fabric, the protests moved him deeply. He described going to Kaplan, the street in Tel Aviv that had become the center of the demonstrations, and being struck by the mix of people around him. He became ever more impressed when attending the protests in Jerusalem.

"When you'd have a person in a kippah, a rabbi who's a principal of a school, followed by a woman in a hijab, and then followed by some secular person (maybe they had to import them from Tel Aviv, I don't know) I actually felt like, wow, this is what's great about this country. All these completely different people are willing to come out and stand for something together."

The protests went on for months, from January 4, 2023, the night Levin gave a speech announcing his intention to completely remake Israel's legal system, until they were cut short ten months later. Every Saturday night, hundreds of thousands of Israelis filled the streets. They became the longest sustained demonstration in the history of the democratic world. And then, once the Knesset passed the first piece of legislation with the country still on the verge of breaking apart, the government paused. They said they wouldn't do anything more until there was broader national consensus.

"I believed them," Danny said. "I really did believe them. And it felt like a vacation after a horrible illness."

He and his wife went to the Negev for a few days. They sat on a mitzpe (a lookout point) and watched the mountains turn purple as the sun set. They breathed in the night air, the silence of the desert.

"I remember sitting there and thinking: Oh my God, it's so good to just be in Israel again. To love this place again without the weight of all that anger."

That feeling, for the most part, followed him through until he went to sleep on October 6. "I was sobered by an awareness of how callous critical numbers of people could be to the feelings of others in Israeli society. But I was also very proud. We had mostly nonviolently, almost entirely nonviolently, the longest protest in the history of the democratic world. I thought: that's pretty cool. Civil society works here. When the government overreaches, the people push back."

And then came October 7th.

"Saturday morning, October 7th, was the most frightening day of my life," Danny told me. "There were hours where I didn't know if my kids were alive."

He has children and grandchildren scattered across the country. As the news came in – fragmented, terrifying, impossible to verify – he was calling, texting, waiting. The rockets were one thing. The reports of terrorists inside Israel were something else entirely.

"You're sitting there and you don't know what's happening. You don't know if your son is okay, if your grandkids are okay. You're watching videos on Telegram that you can't unsee. And you're thinking: this isn't possible. This can't be happening here."

When I asked him how he felt in those first weeks, his answer surprised me.

"I didn't feel powerless in the first weeks of the war. In fact, I felt the opposite of powerless."

He described what he saw happening around him. Civilian command centers popping up overnight. WhatsApp groups turned into logistics operations. People cooking food and driving it south, collecting equipment, housing displaced families. The reservists who grabbed their guns from their closets and drove toward the border without waiting for orders.

"Huge numbers of reservists showing up at their bases, people not even being with their unit, just saying: okay, I hear there's bad stuff going on, I'm going to go fight. Guys who hadn't been in uniform in years just got in their cars and went south. That did not feel like powerlessness. It felt tragic and enraging, but it didn't feel powerless."

The state had failed, catastrophically, unforgivably. But the people had not.

"The army wasn't there, the government wasn't there, but Israelis were there. Within hours, ordinary people had organized themselves into something functional. That's what I kept thinking about in those first weeks. The state collapsed, but civil society held."

The powerlessness came later.

"I have only recently started to feel powerless here."

When I asked him why, he listed the reasons slowly, the pain still raw: the government chipping away at democracy while the country was exhausted from war. The sense of becoming a "vassal state" to the United States in ways Netanyahu hadn't anticipated. Hamas still dangerous, still alive, still ruling Gaza despite a terrible war. The hostages held for so long in Gaza.

"Ron Gvili had been in their hands for sixteen months. We're the biggest power in the region, we thought we knew who had him, and there was nothing we could do. Nothing. The limitation on power is very sobering. A lot of guys with Kalashnikovs and sneakers can do a lot of really, really bad things, and bombing their civilization back to the Stone Age kind of doesn't do any good."

But his powerlessness extends beyond Israel's ability to influence its adversaries and neighbors. Through the conversation I understood that his sense of power and powerlessness is determined primarily by how he feels the government takes his needs into account, whether he believes the leadership is responsive to and responsible for the welfare of Israeli society as a whole. How that government interacts with others on his behalf.

"I feel powerless vis-à-vis Bibi. I feel powerless vis-à-vis the United States. I feel powerless vis-à-vis the wave of antisemitism creeping across Europe."

And then he told me about Josh Shapiro.

"We're having this conversation on January 19th, the day we heard that the governor of Pennsylvania was asked, when he was being vetted as a possible running mate for Kamala Harris, whether or not he'd been a double agent for Israel. What a sickening reprise of old themes of Jewish life."

And yet, he said, there was a bitter irony to it all.

"I would say that the most effective case for Zionism is being made right now by the antisemites of the world. The hatred that is seeping out of the pores of western civilization right now, that unfortunately is sweeping up a lot of very well-intentioned young people who have absolutely no idea that they're being played for fools, is doing more for the Zionist case than anybody could possibly have imagined. And I think that's very sad. But there it is."

And this is why Danny says that he finally understands what it feels like to be a Jew. Why he said that for the first time in his life he understood Jewish history not as history but as present.

"The first 64 years of my life, life was good. There were terrible prime ministers, there were terrible presidents. There were some nasty things done to the Jews here and there. But I felt: wow, look at us compared to the middle of the 20th century. Look how far we've come."

He paused.

"And I feel all of a sudden: oh, now I get what it felt like to be a European Jew. Everybody suspects you of something. Nobody will really be certain to protect you. At the end of the day, some of it's because of your own foolish leadership, some of it's because of mistakes you've made very publicly. And a lot of it has nothing to do with anything other than the fact that you refuse to stop existing."

He told me about his grandmother, his Savta, and her lifelong distrust of non-Jews. She had come from the old world, from the kind of place where Jews learned early not to rely on anyone's goodwill.

"She had three children who were all accomplished professionals living in suburban America, and she never trusted 'the goyim,' as she would put it. Never. I used to be embarrassed about that. I used to say to myself: Savta, it's different now. We live in America. Things have changed. And she would say to me, 'You're so cute'—which meant you're stupid. But she wasn't going to say that I was stupid because I was her only daughter's eldest son. So she'd say 'you're cute,' which I wasn't."

He laughed a little.

"I understand her better now. I really do. All that wariness she carried, all that suspicion—it wasn't paranoia. It was experience. She knew something I didn't."

As did generations of Jews before her. This hit him hard one morning as he recited Tachanun, the penitential prayers observant Jews say each morning, recounting a litany of suffering and disasters that stretches back millennia, and beg God not to let them happen again.

"When I read Tachanun in the morning, you know, 'don't let these terrible things happen to us,' listing things that happened to us over and over again, it used to feel like a quaint little barnstorming of Jewish history. I felt like going through a Jewish history exhibit in a museum very quickly. Okay, we did our little Tachanun thing, so we've done Jewish history in a thumbnail, and now we go on with our day."

He paused.

"It doesn't feel quaint to me anymore. I say it sometimes with my eyes welling up. These people wrote those words hundreds of years ago, begging God to protect us from precisely what's happening now. And look at us, once again, exactly the same thing. The same hatred. The same vulnerability. The same prayers." That is when the powerlessness kicks in, because we should have had a State to protect us, we should have a State that reflects our needs, that empowers us, that cares about how we feel and how we are seen and related to.

And that is when I asked Danny about the destruction of Gaza, because nothing, in my opinion, stands in such stark contrast to Jewish powerlessness than the ultimate application of Jewish power. I asked him whether he thought it was justified, whether he felt guilt, whether he knew what to make of the images.

"I'm just overwhelmed by how much I don't know," he said. "And how small I feel."

He told me he hadn't read Peter Beinart's book, the one that inspired me to write this one, or former speaker of the Knesset (and religious Zionist) Avraham Burg's essay claiming that the destruction of Gaza has led to the destruction of

Jewish civilization, an erasure of all we learned in our long millennia in Exile (though Burg, he noted, is a member of his extended family through his son-in-law. He said he admires Burg's intellectual acuity and moral courage, even though they disagree about virtually everything).

"I don't buy this notion that this was the end of Jewish civilization. I think that's silly. Even if we did more than we should have in Gaza, it's not the end of Jewish civilization. It's just not."

Jewish civilization, Danny stated, is more than just our years of powerlessness, our attempts to cope with our position in a world not ours, the philosophies and laws we enacted to protect ourselves and hold together our communities while dispersed among the nations. Jewish civilization is greater than that. It has just as much memory of power and kingdom and sovereignty as it does of powerlessness and dispersion. Let's remember, David beat Goliath, not by debate but by the use of violence, and he then went on to take over the Jewish Kingdom and expand its borders.

But that doesn't mean he believes that what happened in Gaza can be ignored. "I don't know what percentage of buildings were really destroyed. I don't know what percentage of those buildings needed to be destroyed. I don't know that anybody in the army actually knows, because there are so many different pockets of people doing all different sorts of things." What he does know is that we can't look away. "Part of me says:

wow, this is pretty horrible. Unspeakable. I don't know what to make of that picture."

He paused.

"But yeah, don't screw with us anymore. That's part of the lesson of the twentieth and twenty-first century. That voice is in there too, and I'm not going to pretend it isn't."

And so I asked him, given this complexity, this weight, this feeling of powerlessness yet pride at being able to stand up for ourselves, where does he find hope?

It's the National Library.

"I like to go every now and then to the National Library to work for the day, just to change the venue. If you don't get there by 9:30, 10 o'clock, you're not getting a seat." He laughs. "I love that. In an era when everybody's telling you that you don't need libraries anymore, 'why'd you build this big fancy building by world-renowned European architects that cost a gazillion dollars, nobody needs libraries anymore,' and you can't get a seat. Every seat is taken. Every table is full."

He described what he sees in the reading room. The building is new, designed by Herzog & de Meuron, all light and space and calm and quiet. But what fills it is old, ancient: books and manuscripts, the accumulated wisdom of Jewish civilization, humanity in its dispersion.

"It's just so cool to go to the capital of the Jewish state, in the National Library, and be there with Haredim and with people who are tattooed everywhere you can see and women, Haredi women with their heads covered in dresses down to the floor, and women in the summer wearing spaghetti straps and shorts, and everybody's sharing the same tables because that's just how it rolls there. And we're all surrounded by the books in the reading room."

He took a moment, as if envisioning the room.

"I sometimes just sit back and look, and I go: wow. Like, that's really unbelievable. All these completely different Jews, who probably can't stand each other politically, sitting together in silence, reading. And it makes me proud, and it gives me hope."

I asked him whether that was enough to fight back his feeling of powerlessness, to counter the sense of betrayal by the government, and the sense of siege from the world. Whether hope drawn from a library building could sustain him.

"People can probably chuckle and say: if you need to draw your hope from a library building in the face of all the other garbage you've just laid out, then you're kind of desperate."

He smiled.

"Maybe. But maybe not. Maybe it's the magic of the book and the belief in something ethereal and everlasting that's what's kept us going. And if we're in a period of darkness and shortsightedness and power-grabbingness, okay, but maybe one day the clouds will clear and the sun will shine through, and we can recreate something that the world will once again look at with admiration. Not only for our tech, not only because we can do something with drones that nobody else in the world can do, but for other things."

He told me about a trip he'd taken to the Negev a few days before our conversation. A group of Shalem College graduates had organized a gathering in one of the small communities in the south. Young couples with kids, working in high tech, all planning to move to the periphery.

"These kids are smart," he said. "They understand the darkness. They've lived through all of it: the protests, the war, the hostages, the international hatred. And they're not going anywhere. They're not leaving Israel. They're not moving to the center where it's safer and easier. They're moving to the Negev. They're having kids. They're building something."

He leaned back.

"If books and ideas hadn't kept the Jewish people alive for a very long time, we wouldn't be here. So what kind of Jewish discourse, what kind of conversation that's not based entirely on power and certainty, can we build in this country that will make our children and grandchildren want to be part of it?"

That story spoke to me in particular as a person who cares about ideas, and who believes in the importance of dialogue and discussion in shaping community. Because, as I've come to understand, that which connects individuals and turns them into a family, a household, a community, a nation, is the narrative they share about their past, their present, and their future. Words matter because they communicate the position each person takes in that narrative. They indicate whether a person is either inside the story or outside of it.

The other thing that stayed with me after my conversation with Danny was the realization that the powerlessness many of us felt after October 7th came less from the attacks and more from how our government responded to them. How it took hours for the military to send down troops to secure our homes. How it took days, even weeks, for ministries to function. The social contract between Israeli citizens and the state had been shattered that morning. What emerged in its place was something else: a deeper and more profound trust between Israelis, a stubborn insistence on showing up for each other, replacing the role of government to become a de facto government by the people and for the people.

Yet the longer the war raged, and the more destructive it became, the more the government returned to the fore, and the more powerless many of us felt. The more we realized that the answer to bad government cannot be civil society alone. The shattering of our social contract demands more than the building of new communities. It requires new ideas.

Alina Shkolnikov

There is a particular moment that Alina Shkolnikov thinks about when she thinks about the Second Intifada. She was a teenager in Pisgat Ze'ev, a neighborhood in the north of Jerusalem, and she was at a Seeds of Peace dialogue session, the kind of coexistence meeting that people in her neighborhood treated as either naïve or treasonous. She decided to attend, testing the limits of her own politics, just to see what it was about. It was there a young Palestinian man she had come to know through the session told her about his cousin. Their age. Killed by an Israeli sniper in what he described as a "wandering bullet."

"It completely changed everything that I thought in my life to that moment," she told me. "Something happens and all of a sudden you're like, wow, there are people dying on the other side of this conflict."

I asked her what she had thought before that moment.

"My perspective before was of an absolute right and an absolute wrong, and us being absolute right. Having the moral high ground to...I told people it needs to be gone. Gaza needs to be gone. The Palestinian cities around Jerusalem need to be gone. Flattened. I said it without remorse, that the only way to make it gone is to make it disappear. To make the intifada and the wars and the death stop."

As a teenager living in Pisgat Ze'ev, that was the world she knew, and that sentiment remains common in her childhood neighborhood today, because they grew up learning that force was the only true arbiter. Democracy was at best second to freedom from fear. The idea that someone her age died on the other side of the conflict, the recognition of the humanity of the person, seeing a human not as a statistic, not as an abstraction, but as a boy with a name – who had a cousin who was sitting across from her – had not occurred to her. Not really. Not with a face, a name, a life story. "That moment I realized: we are all dying for this conflict."

The difference between knowing there is death as a consequence of a struggle and knowing that someone human has been killed and they and their family will never see them again for no fault of their own, changed her. She did not abandon her politics, not yet. She did not flip her identity. She widened it. She found she could hold another story alongside her own without the two destroying each other. This was her first reconciliation with the greater world, when the wall around a single narrative cracked open and she looked through.

She has been looking through ever since. And what she has seen in the two years since October 7th, since the collapse of Israel's sense of security, the terrible attacks, the war, the devastation in Gaza, has challenged her once again.

To understand what October 7th did to Alina, you have to first understand what it means to grow up a Soviet Jew.

Her grandparents lived with her family in their multigenerational home in Pisgat Ze'ev. Her grandfather had what she called "the look" — he was Jewish in a way that was visible, that could not be hidden, that drew comments from his Ukrainian neighbors drunk enough to say what they would not say sober. Growing up in his house, surrounded by his stories and the rest of her family – about violent antisemitism and straightforward discrimination – Alina absorbed a lesson she did not have to articulate because it was as ever present as the weather: antisemitism exists. It is always there. It will not disappear because you are educated, because your neighbor seems friendly, because the constitution says otherwise.

"In Russian, you can say: if there's no water in the faucet, it's because of the Jews (it rhymes in Russian, I promise). And it's not even said as a sad thing, it's not even a "racist" thing to say. It's just...it is. It's a part of your being, this element of pure racism. Your neighbor's a little bit drunk, so now he's going to tell you whatever it is he wants to tell you about your face."

What this produces is not fear, not exactly. It's more of a tuning, a calibration, to the injustices of the world, a hardened cynicism always ready for action. Soviet Jews do not expect safety. The expectation simply does not exist. American Jews, she believes, have a different experience of reality, made comfortable by nearly a century of tolerance, of increasing inclusion, by decades of relative comfort, into thinking safety is their birthright.

"That's the difference between Soviet Jewry and American Jewry. American Jewry thinks that they are safe for whatever reason, and we know that we're not. And we don't have expectations. There's no expectation."

She had carried this calibration her whole life. Through the Second Intifada, through the second Lebanon War, through all of the battles and wars with Hamas ruling Gaza since. She had never felt unsafe inside Israel, at least not in the deeper foundational sense. She had fear, she heard sirens, she saw the buses blow up and cafes demolished by suicide bombers. She felt what she calls normal Israeli anxiety. But she didn't share the fundamental feeling of distrust of her fellow citizens and her government felt by Soviet Jews in the Former Soviet Union because she was Israeli: The army existed. The army would come to save her even if it meant hurting others.

And then October 7th happened. And nobody came.

"That was my biggest heartbreak. The first week. Where was the saving? That broke me."

She quickly thought about the implications, emotionally and logistically. She thought about what would have happened if the attack had come not from Gaza but from Judea and Samaria, from the villages that nearly touch Pisgat Ze'ev. Who would have arrived? Magav (the border police unit)? The local police? Would anyone have come at all?

"That thought, that nobody's coming, is terrifying inside Israel. The concept of safety shattered for me in totality."

The Soviet in her had never expected safety outside Israel. That was settled knowledge. But she had expected it in Israel. And when that promise was broken, she was broken.

Alina is, by her own accounting, Israeli first and Soviet Jew second. She served two years as the Head of the Russian Desk at the IDF spokesperson unit, spent two years saying, publicly and officially, that the army will always be there to defend Israel, that we are the most moral army in the world. I met her after her service, after her academic degree, when she joined PresenTense to direct our operations in the former Soviet Union. Alina has a unique fluency in Hebrew, Russian, and English – linguistically and culturally and cognitively, able to bridge between individuals and communities and translate pedagogy to fit the mindset of each community she worked with. I learned so much from her then, and continue to learn so much from her since.

A few years ago she moved with her husband, Dimitry, also a Soviet Jew, to New York, where his job took him, and she continues to work in bridging worlds. I describe her background this way because her experience is shared by many immigrants who continue to feel Israel is their home, even if they no longer live there themselves.

For Alina, and for others I've spoken with, the best metaphor they could use to describe their feeling of abandonment on October 7th was the metaphor of an adult child recognizing the imperfection of their parents. Many of the people I spoke with said: I know my parents are just human. I grew up and realized they weren't perfect, that they make mistakes. I still love them, but now I see clearly how badly they failed.

Alina took it to the extreme.

"It's not that you just woke up and found out your parents are shit. It's that you woke up and found out that your parents...that your father murdered your mother. That is what it felt like with the army and the government. You found out that the two entities you trusted most all of your life, and gave service to — not just trusted, no, supported, participated in, were, that they were nothing. It felt like," she said, carefully, hesitantly, witnessing "the murder-suicide of your parents."

Hearing that shocked me into silence. The more I thought about it, the more it made me understand the deep pain the weeks after October 7th caused to the Israeli psyche. Why for so many Israelis today the failures of October 7th are not just categorized as the failures of inept or corrupt politicians. It's more than that. It feels like a betrayal by the very people we counted on to protect us, who we were willing to sacrifice ourselves for. A betrayal by the institutions we gave years of our life to, staked our safety on, had spoken for publicly. A bewilderment that those institutions – that those people who embody those institutions – had failed at the precise moment we needed the most.

And then came the war in Gaza, and, for Alina in particular, the betrayal deepened.

"I feel deeply uncomfortable — deep, like to the core of my being, to the shame of my soul — about some of what is reported we have done, and horrified that we feel we are entitled to do whatever we want."

She said this carefully. Not as someone performing anguish, not as someone seeking absolution, but as someone reporting a condition they have been living with and have no intention of looking away from. The shame of her soul. "I'm a person of extreme ownership," she shared, "so there's very little I put on other people. I have no control over what Hamas does. I should have absolute control — not me, as an individual, but we — over how we handle ourselves. And we failed."

When she says "we failed," she includes herself, even if she lives in the US at the moment. When Alina says "we," she means it the way a doctor means "we" when delivering bad news about a patient to a family member. Not as an excuse. As a recognition of accountability. And that responsibility does not stop on October 7th. It extends all the way through. Into the war. Into Gaza.

She believes the reckoning is coming. She believes most Israelis do not yet know, not fully, what has been done in their name.

"When the borders will open to journalists, we are going to have a moment of awakening like no other."

I asked her what she thought that awakening would look like. She was quiet for a moment.

"I don't know. But I've seen it before, in smaller ways, with smaller things. And the bigger the thing, the more the awakening shakes you. What happened in Gaza is not a small thing."

She is not saying Israel intended genocide. She does not believe that is true, even if some of the terrible politicians she blames for the rupture may have wished it. She is saying the distinction may not be the moral center of gravity she once thought it was. What matters is what we did. And she believes that there will come a time when we need to face the facts.

"We really like saying: those American kids on campus, they're so brainwashed. But we're just as brainwashed. We are all brainwashed. And we really want to have a single narrative that says: I am good, you are bad. If I am good and you are bad, I can do no harm to you. If I do any harm to you or your children, that's okay, because I am good and you are bad. And if you cry for help and I don't reach to help you, that's okay because you hurt me first. And if your neighbor by proxy who lives next to you is also hurt in a way because I'm hurting you, that's okay because they chose to live next to you."

This is how a society makes peace with things it could not otherwise live with. Nobody wakes up and decides to be a perpetrator. What happens is they decide not to define what they do as the thing they condemn. And thus they install an internal permission structure, brick by brick, over months and years, until a wall of justifications is so complete one cannot see through it. Until someone's death is not seen for what it is: the ending of a human life.

She watched this happen inside herself.

"The past two years have crystallized for me what Yeshayahu Leibowitz warned about, the corruption of the occupier. I feel how we have let fear seep into us, how we let our anger seep into us, how we let our hearts go dark. And if our heart is dark then you just Other more and more and more. When you have no empathy, you literally cannot see the Other."

Leibowitz, an Israeli Orthodox Rabbi, a spiritual leader and critic of the then-government's policies, spoke and wrote fifty years ago about the corruption that would come to the Israeli psyche if we were to keep our control of the territories captured in the war of 1967, and rule over the Palestinians without integrating them into Israeli society. He was dismissed as an alarmist and a provocateur. Alina has been watching his prophecy unfold, and the thing she finds most frightening is the invisibility of the corruption to Israeli society.

Rabbi Mijal Bitton taught Alina a concept years before any of this that she thinks is especially relevant to Israelis now, a concept she has carried ever since: "second naïveté" (or reconciliation).

Not reconciliation between enemies. The internal kind. The kind that happens when something you once held as an absolute truth cracks open, and you have to find your way back to a new relationship with the idea.

"You believe in God," Alina explained. "Then you have a crisis of faith. Then you believe in God again. And that faith, the return to having faith in something that you hadn't for a while, is different from the first one. It applies to everything. Whatever it is you think is a philosophical concept, an absolute truth. You have a moment where you didn't think it's true anymore, and then you come to it again."

On October 6, 2023, she was already in the middle of such a reconciliation with Zionism. She had questions she had not finished asking. She had gone on maternity leave (her son had just been born) and had read Theodor Herzl's *Altneuland* anew. The experience had shaken her.

"I read in the midst of the judicial reform and said: why didn't we do this? There was something very simple there: a state very deeply rooted in Judaism on one hand. On the other hand, very pluralistic, very accepting of differences with non-Jewish heroes in the text. In the original vision there was room for everyone and for multiple narratives, and everything runs as it should. Yes, it's fiction but it's a vision of what we were supposed to be."

What stunned her was not the utopian quality but the specificity of the pluralism Herzl had imagined for what the Jewish State could become. How his imagined state treated its minorities, how it understood what Jewish self-determination actually required of the Jews themselves. It was not an afterthought in the text. It was in the architecture.

"Are we living Herzl's vision? A hundred percent no. Do we need to revive the vision? A hundred percent yes. We had a path and then we went completely off it. Now we're just deteriorating towards something. We need to find a new path."

The attacks, the absolute failure of the government and the army, the heartless destruction of Gaza, all of these did not obviate her reconciliation with Zionism. They made it more urgent. She is not disappointed with the project. She is disappointed with what is being practiced in its name, and with the fact that almost no one arguing about it, on any side, has read its source.

"The Zionist idea from the get-go is the idea of a national state. I believe that we need to have our own national state and Palestinians need to have their own ethnic state. Not just deserve it – we both need it. If I believe I should get a state, you should get a state. Whatever the definition of 'you' is. In Judaism that is the whole idea of Tikkun Olam: it's not just for us, it's always for the greater of humanity."

Her argument cuts through both dominant positions, pro- and antizionist: if you oppose the ethnostate in principle, you must oppose it everywhere. Including Palestine. But if you support the idea that people who have come together out of a shared feeling of belonging, out of a desire to determine their destiny collectively and express their values through political action, then you should support others to do the same.

The progressive critics who frame Israel as uniquely colonial, uniquely sinister, have not followed their own principle to its conclusion: just as the Palestinians deserve to determine their destiny, so do the Jews who have sought a home of their own for thousands of years. Same with the Israeli right which has distorted Zionism into a license for dominance — claiming 'our state, our democracy, we can do what we want' — which is in flat out contradiction to the founding values of the movement they claim to represent. Neither extreme has truly wrestled with the implications of forcing people who reject their vision, who do not feel they belong in either absolute. Because there is the practical matter of millions of people who live on a piece of land who will not go anywhere or give up their right to self-determination just because someone else believes they should.

So, given that Israel exists, and Israelis will not leave, and neither will the Palestinians, what does she recommend people who reject Israel's current direction do?

"You believe that the State of Israel can do better? Great. Donate to the democratic organizations you think are going to make it better. You think Jewish organizations should work on the recovery of Gaza? I think so too. Great. You're worried about what's safe and mistrust iNGOs [international non-governmental organizations]? Put money in aid organizations that are Israeli. You think there needs to be better education for democracy in Israel? Great. Put your money in organizations."

There is a civil society in Israel, she says, that would flourish if critics of Israel would choose to engage with it seriously. The Right has been funding Israeli political infrastructure for a decade. Too much of the Left – liberal and progressive alike – has stood back, criticizing without engaging, seeking to keep its hands clean, afraid to get involved. Arguing whether or not to adopt or abandon the label of Zionism. As if labeling themselves one way or another would make a difference in the reconstruction of Gaza, in the defense of Israel's liberal democracy.

I had to admit to her at that point that I was finding it hard reconciling how she could feel so betrayed by the State, on one hand, and yet remain so motivated to advocate for those outside of the State to continue to support it. So I asked: how could she advocate for a project that shamed her so thoroughly?

"It's still a speck in history," she said. "Hopefully in the next two hundred years, if AI doesn't kill us by then, we'll be able to look back and say: remember that dark period in our history when we killed each other. Isn't it great that we're no longer there? We are in chapter three of a very long book."

That made sense to me. The shame Alina felt when witnessing the destruction of Gaza does not give her a reason to give up on the project. Quite the opposite, it is an indication to her that she needs to own it and get more deeply involved. It serves as evidence that the project is unfinished, that the Zionism being practiced is not the Zionism that was imagined, and that someone has to hold both truths at once. She hopes this for both Israelis and Palestinians.

"Think about what it meant for Israelis to make peace with Germany," she said. "Not just a government signing a paper, but people, actual people, deciding that their children would grow up in a different relationship with that history. That didn't happen in a year. It didn't happen in a generation. We are asking something similar now, and we think it should be resolved in a news cycle."

She reminded me that reconciliation between the Germans and the Jews began less than five years after the last concentration camp was emptied. She invoked the Irish and the English, the Scandinavian wars, the long violent centuries that preceded what are now among the most stable societies on earth. The historical record of peoples who have tried to kill each other and then, eventually, found a different arrangement. Not because they forgot, or because justice was fully served, but because the alternative of permanent war, permanent dehumanization, permanent refusal to see the other side as human, was worse. She is not naive about what this requires. She is no stranger to a conflict that makes such comparisons seem obscene to people on both sides. She makes them anyway.

Which is why she believes that a better future is possible, if we dedicate ourselves to bringing it about.

"The best case scenario: a rebuilt Middle East. Not just Israel and Palestine, the whole region, Middle East and North Africa, with religion at its core rather than at its throat. An Abrahamic union of nations, each with their own character, bound by economic interdependence and something shared and acknowledged. A two-state solution as the floor, not the ceiling. And Gaza and the Gaza envelope, and the north of

Israel and the south of Lebanon as the greatest reconstruction projects in modern history."

She said this last part with something that I can only describe as practicality. Not pathos. Not wishful thinking. As the logical thing humans should do given that larger reconstruction projects have been successfully carried out repeatedly in our remembered history.

But that takes commitment. It requires a dedication to the very state that failed us, that shamed us. It requires partners. It requires patience. "You can't look at chapter three," I keep hearing Alina say, "and be like, I'm done with this book."

David Green

David B. Green was my editor at Haaretz English Edition, where I contributed opinion pieces early on in my time in Israel. David shaped, trimmed and sharpened them, pushing back when my arguments were sloppy.

David is a journalist by profession, but David is also something else: a lifelong activist for equal rights inside Israel, a man who grew up in Hashomer Hatzair in the United States. As a writer, he has spent decades arguing that the country's treatment of its Arab citizens is the measure of its democracy. I have always admired his writing, his precision, and the particular quality of his convictions: deeply left-wing, deeply Zionist, deeply uncomfortable with the gap between the two.

David remembers sleeping fitfully on the morning of October 7th, as is often the case for him. By 4:30 or 5, he was already awake, and trying to drift back to sleep. At 6:30, when the missile alerts began sounding, he turned on the radio. The news filtered in slowly. It was an hour or two before it became apparent that something extraordinary was taking place. He came to realize that this wasn't just another terror attack, not simply a case of a single community being invaded, which had previously been an Israeli worst-case scenario. Rather, an entire area along the border had been overrun.

David lives in Jerusalem, a city that is very rarely the target for missiles. There is a kind of assumption, he said, that the city is safe because one-third of its population is Arab, and Muslim states apparently are not comfortable shooting at a city where they risk hitting Arab victims or Muslim shrines. That didn't stop him from spending most of the day in front of the television, absorbing what was happening as information trickled in. But he recalls that it took a few days, maybe a week, to grasp the full number of communities involved, and the cruelty of the attacks.

I asked him whether, as the scope of what had happened became clear, he felt a sense of powerlessness, a reawakening of a vestigial, historical feeling of Jewish vulnerability, as was the case with others I had spoken with.

No, he told me.

"The actual tactics that they used to overwhelm our defenses, enabling them to cross the border in such huge numbers, and to cause the damage that they did, were shocking. But none of it was really surprising to me. It didn't change my expectation that Israel would be able to bounce back and repel the invasion."

This is the distinction that defined everything David said to me over the course of our conversation. October 7th, for him, did not symbolize, even temporarily, a return to Jewish powerlessness. It was a failure of competence. The failure of an army and a government that had closed their eyes to a reality that was always going to catch up with them. He thinks about

October 7th from a position of empowerment, not fear. And this, David insisted, is what Zionism was supposed to mean. Not victimhood. Not being under siege. The confidence of power. The capacity to take initiative, to shape events, to act rather than merely react.

Zionism was the project of turning Jews from objects of history into authors of it. What he saw in the current government was a betrayal of that founding idea: a leadership that had all the power of a sovereign state and used it only to manage, to deter, to intimidate; never to build, never to negotiate, never to imagine.

David initially hoped the crisis would force a fundamental rethinking among the country's elites. He had hoped the same thing a year earlier, during the initial stages of the judicial reform crisis. He imagined, naively he now admits, that the energy that had brought hundreds of thousands into the streets to protest the government's assault on democracy might now be directed at the deeper strategic failure: the government's decades-long strategy of not acknowledging the contradiction between Israel's claim to be a model democracy and its being an occupier.

"It was clear to me that Israel had to respond militarily and that it would. But I really bought into the belief pretty quickly that this was an opportunity for positive change. This was a crisis, after all, and it should have thrown into question our country's entire strategic vision and policies. And thus, maybe finally, I hoped, we would be sufficiently shaken that we, both our government and our people, would take advantage of the opportunity to make a fundamental, strategic change in the way we related to our neighbors, because it couldn't go on this way."

Instead of awakening people to the reality that our neighbors would not be going away and that it was time to invest in ways of solving the conflict between us, much of the Israeli public was led to believe differently.

"People's eyes were 'opened,' as was being said at the time. But what they were opened to was the understanding that there is no solution. That this is not a problem that can be solved."

David was disappointed, if not shocked, by this response. He told me about knowledgeable experts on Palestinian society – people who had previously identified with the Left – who told him in the months after October 7th that the event had changed everything for them. That they now understood that Arabs and Jews had fundamentally different understandings of the world. That they would never be able to live together in mutual security.

But for David, this was obviously, demonstrably wrong. Palestinian citizens of Israel had been living alongside Jewish Israelis in peace for 77 years, despite not being treated equally, despite not having the same opportunities.

"The fact that for almost 80 years, the Palestinian citizens of Israel have lived basically in peace with the Jewish majority, with constantly improving material conditions and rights and opportunities, I think that that's almost miraculous, considering that we're still at war with their nation, their people."

He rejects the idea that there are irreconcilable civilizational differences between Israelis and Palestinians because the evidence is unimpeachable: the Palestinians on the Israeli side of the Green Line (the armistice line that separated Israeli troops from Jordanian and Egyptian troops at the end of the 1948 war) are the same people, from the same families, same tribes, as those living in the territories. It makes no logical sense to imagine that people on one side can be model citizens, while people on the other side will always remain mortal enemies.

"Of course there are cultural differences, and differences in values and so forth. But people want more or less the same thing. Most people."

He drew a sharp line, however, at Hamas. Hamas had to be overcome. Not because all Palestinians were the enemy, but precisely because Hamas was the exception that had been allowed to define the rule.

"I think that Hamas – and Islamist fundamentalism in general – is an enemy with whom we cannot make peace. They're not interested in the same things as I think most people are, and they are possessed by an ideology that is extremist and uncompromising and simply doesn't see room for the Jews here. But that should have been clear even before October 7th."

Hamas could not be a partner for peace because their rejection of Israel is an essential component of their identity. And yet, it was that rejection of Israel in any form that led to successive governments led by Netanyahu to support Hamas financially and politically. That way, as has been widely reported based on Netanyahu's own statements in closed-door sessions, he could ensure that his political camp always had an excuse to avoid any progress toward an agreed upon pathway to Palestinian self-determination.

But Hamas was and remains only a small proportion of the Palestinian population, ruling Gaza with an iron fist. Treating the entire population as if it were Hamas, conflating the ideology of an extremist group with human nature itself, is precisely the error that made so many believe that resolution of the conflict is impossible. In many ways, it even guaranteed it.

What's needed, David said, is a more holistic vision. It was foolish to think that Israel could go into Gaza and destroy Hamas purely by military means. For one, the group had prepared for an invasion, with tunnels, fortified positions, fighters embedded in the civilian population. And of course, even if Israel could have succeeded in killing every single member of Hamas and its sister jihadist groups, without changing the overall situation, more would arise in their wake. Or, more precisely, more would be nurtured by interested parties who want to perpetuate the conflict between Arabs and Jews.

What October 7th revealed, David said, was not a new threat but the price of an old delusion. For decades, and especially in the last two decades under the leadership of

Netanyahu and his successive governments, Israel had been living in what he saw as a state of unreality.

"We've been lulled into a sense of complacency because for the past decade or so, we have lived high on the hog while paying a minimal price on the security level. And people have closed their eyes to the reality of our situation vis-à-vis the Palestinians, and to the price we're paying internally in terms of the deterioration of our moral state, our norms, our ethics."

Not everything can be blamed on Netanyahu.

"You could go back to the 'Disengagement' of 20 years ago, but I would go back to 1967. What was supposed to be a temporary situation became a permanent one. And you can't claim otherwise after almost 60 years."

The policy of isolating Gaza after Ariel Sharon's 2005 Disengagement, when Israel pulled out both army and settlers unilaterally and then, after the takeover by Hamas in 2007, sealed the territory, had created the perfect environment for the empowerment of Hamas. Israel had chosen not to engage, not to negotiate, not to build an alternative to Hamas. And then Israel acted surprised when Hamas did what it said it would do, what it regularly declared it would do to anyone who would listen.

It was only natural for Israel's first response to that surprise to be in kind.

"We had to deter additional attacks. And I think human nature is such that we had to have vengeance for the attacks. We had to respond and do damage and destruction for our own sense of satisfaction, and that's a very, very human need. I'm not so naive as to deny that."

But it was widely known from the beginning that just killing Hamas would not solve the problem. The former chief of staff and defense minister Moshe "Bogie" Ya'alon told David that by the beginning of 2024, Israel had accomplished the strategic goals that could be accomplished militarily. Yair Golan, the former general who now leads Israel's Democratic party, said the same. What was needed was a political vision, a plan for what came after the fighting. "No such plan existed, because Netanyahu never considered that as a possibility. All he talked about was total victory without ever defining what total victory was."

And then came the Trump plan for turning Gaza into a Riviera, a luxury sea-side real estate development. Netanyahu's enthusiastic response to the suggestion that all Palestinian residents of Gaza could be removed, the territory rebuilt, and maybe a few of them allowed back in ten years, struck David as the clearest evidence of the unreality.

"The fact that Netanyahu said, yeah, great idea, we're for that. And the whole cabinet said that was a great idea. That's evidence to me that we're completely unrealistic and unwilling to confront the situation that we're in. It's just unreal. And it's also not moral."

This whole time a different offer was on the table, placed there at the beginning of the war by Saudi Arabia, the Gulf states, and the Arab League. In fact, the Arab League's peace plan, which included recognition and acceptance of Israel in exchange for an end to the military occupation and the establishment of a Palestinian state, had been around since 2002. It had never been withdrawn. But in Israel it had never even been considered as a starting point for negotiation.

"Instead, we've allowed ourselves to accept that there's no solution and there's nothing to be done. And we're the victims here because, by our understanding, we have this relentless foe that will never accept us. But in fact, we are the ones who have over time become the relentless party that is unwilling to even acknowledge or accept the possibility that maybe there is a solution. Nobody has the right, vis-à-vis their children, to just throw up their hands and say, we're going to live by the sword forever."

This is where David introduced an argument that resonates with me: Israel's victim mentality and the self-perception of weakness that was strangling the country's capacity to act. David acknowledged that the victim mentality had genuine roots. Israel in its early years really was insecure. The existential threats were real: the War of Independence, the Six-Day War, the Yom Kippur War. A Palestinian national movement that was uncompromisingly committed to eliminating Israel. But the past several decades had seen Israel transform into a regional power – militarily dominant, economically self-reliant, recognized diplomatically by most of the world's states. Self-perception, however, had not caught up with reality.

"Our leading politicians and most of its citizens have continued to perceive Israel as weak, as a potential victim that must remain perpetually vigilant. And I think that self-perception is what is ultimately going to destroy Israel, which is to say, make it unrecognizable."

This, David insisted, was fundamentally a failure of leadership. People could be helped to see that the country they lived in was not the beleaguered outpost of 1948. It is time Israelis recognized that Israel is a powerful state with the agency to shape its own future. But that requires leaders willing to tell the truth, and the current leadership is willing to do anything but.

Listening to him, I thought about the dynamic I had observed throughout this war: the more the world condemned Israel, the more Israelis retreated into the victim narrative, which in turn made it impossible to seize the diplomatic openings sitting on the table. The victim mentality and the strongman ideology that propped up Netanyahu fed each other. As long as enough Israelis felt the siege was real, there was no room for the conversation David wanted to have.

I found myself thinking something that may sound callous, but the more I think about it the more I wonder whether it is true: perhaps the destruction of Gaza, as terrible as it was, will over time serve as the lesson Israel needed. Not a lesson in restraint, or in the limits of power, but a lesson in what it means to have power, period. Overwhelming power. The final acknowledgment that Zionism has succeeded. That there is no longer any doubt that Israel is not a dream or a proposition or a fragile experiment. It is a state, a military power, a regional force that reshaped the map of the Middle East in the space of a little over two years.

We are no longer victims. We are historic actors with power beyond anything the Jews of exile could have imagined. The answer to the destruction of Gaza is not less power, it is not for Jews to give up their state in exchange for a return to the historic position of the victim, but rather a fuller embodiment of power. Ownership of our position, or capabilities. The confidence to negotiate from strength. The confidence to accept offers. The confidence to heal the fear that stemmed from centuries of powerlessness, to stop reacting from trauma and start acting from agency. Power itself is not evil. It can enable one to do good. But only if one knows one has it and is not afraid of losing it, or using it when necessary.

An Israel that recognizes its power can have the hard conversations that an Israel under siege cannot. For David, the questions that need to be addressed include: "What does it mean to be an Israeli citizen? What are your responsibilities? And what are your rights? And how far do your rights go? We've had one government after another that for its own political survival has been willing to bury those questions in order to make coalitions that will keep it in power. And everyone knows, though some won't admit it, that it can't go on this way."

These questions are especially pressing for Israel's Arab citizens, some of whom consider themselves Palestinian-Israelis. David has spent a lot of time talking with this community, including after October 7th, and what has always struck him is the asymmetry of knowledge each community has about the other.

"Almost across the board, Israeli Palestinians know us Jews better than we know them because they move in our society, and they can read and speak Hebrew, and they are exposed to the Hebrew media. And we have much less understanding of them because most of us, me included, don't know Arabic, and we have minimal contact with Arabs, certainly not on a social level."

"I've become increasingly uncomfortable over the years with the lack of equal citizenship and equal rights of Israeli Jews and Israeli Palestinian citizens."

David's sense is that, overall, Israel's Arabs accept living in a Jewish state, and yearn for greater integration into Israeli society. Much of blame for the continued disconnect and mutual suspicion, in his opinion, belongs, again, to the leadership, not the populace. People could be led toward inclusion just as they had been led toward exclusion. He told me about the Future Vision documents, detailed proposals published in 2006 by the Arab Higher Follow-up Committee, which represents the political leadership of Israel's Arab citizens. It was their attempt to present a vision of an acceptable arrangement between Jews and Arabs in the state.

The documents, which indeed had much in them that would be unacceptable to most Jewish Israelis, received a flurry of attention in the media and among Jewish intellectuals and politicians. All of it was negative, with almost no one treating it as a starting point for conversation. No one seemed to recognize the inherent value in the Arab community's having gone through the trouble to draft the program, or to come back with any counter-proposals. In less than a year, the Future Vision documents were forgotten, certainly among the Jewish population.

It was, David said, a lost opportunity, like the Arab League peace plan, like this war. A pattern of refusing to engage with a situation that challenges our understanding of reality, because engaging would mean giving up the victim narrative that justified doing nothing.

I asked David what he wanted Israel to be. He began from first principles.

"What Israel should be is a democracy where all citizens have equal rights. And I think it's possible to have that. It's possible to be a state whose principal language is Hebrew and which follows the Hebrew calendar, celebrating the Jewish holidays as national holidays, for example. Obviously, I don't think religion and politics should mix, and I don't think that any form of religious practice should receive preferential treatment. All of this would be easier to achieve if and when there is a Palestinian national entity, but even within Israel, I think we should be able to agree on the right of this national minority to be recognized as such. In any case, changes have to be arrived at through dialogue and mutual respect, and just because Jews are the majority doesn't mean they should be able to dictate how things are meant to be."

I had to admit that I do find it odd that we are so ready to accept that Jews and Hindus and Muslims feel at home in the United States of America where Christmas and Easter are national holidays and every Starbucks and department store plays carols from Thanksgiving through New Year's, but we somehow reject the notion that non-Jews could feel at home in Israel. Just as Western elites accept that nearly every European country has a cross on their flag, has a state religion, has a culture deeply rooted in an ethnoreligious past, and yet Israel is to be denied that normalcy, and many Europeans and Israelis alike can't imagine that Arabs living in Israel can be as comfortable as Jews have become in the countries of their dispersion.

For David, the reason many if not most Israelis cannot believe that Palestinian identity can coexist with Hebrew and Jewish culture is due to fear. It is because of fear that Jews overcompensate and project what looks like national supremacism. Fear of the other. Fear of change. Fear of losing something. And that fear prevents the advancement of equality.

Instead of focusing on our fear, David said, we should focus on what we love.

"I love Israel. I love the fact that it's a Jewish state, in the sense that I love the Jewish people and their diversity. And I love the quiet of Friday afternoon before Shabbat. And I love the fact that all of these things move me. The music, the culture, even the Jewish people who are very different from me and with whom I might disagree on some very fundamental issues. I still feel that they're my brethren. But I'm equally proud of and appreciative of the fact that we have a free and open enough society that we can also absorb and welcome people who aren't Jews. And I think that instead of moving toward greater acceptance and greater freedom, we're becoming more and more insular and isolated and not even willing to have the big conversations about what we want our state to be."

This, I think, is the thing that people outside Israel (and many inside it) struggle to understand about someone like David. He is one of the smartest critics of the state I know. He has long felt that Israel's treatment of its Arab citizens leaves a lot to be desired, that the occupation of the Palestinian territories is untenable, that the reluctance to look at ourselves critically is self-destructive. And he holds all of these opinions because he loves the country, and believes in its power. Its strength. The fact that it can afford to make hard decisions and compromises, in spite of its fears. He holds Israel to the standard he believes it is capable of meeting, and the gap between the standard and the reality is what drives him to write and act as he has over the years.

"I still believe that we can make a great country together and that we should be able to live with our differences without one group having to dominate the other."

After our conversation I kept thinking about the duality David presented: fear and love. He did not experience October 7th as a revelation of Jewish weakness. He experienced it as a failure of competency in a powerful state that had been lulled into an unrealistic understanding of its situation, distracted by false fears used by political players mainly concerned about maintaining their grip on power. Leaders who thought they could keep kicking the Palestinian can down the road by temporarily supporting the worst elements of Palestinian society financially and politically. A defensive posture that was supposed to be temporary after 1967 and became permanent. The managing of the situation replaced the solving of it. But most of all the victim mentality – the self-perception of weakness in a country that is anything but weak – which has made it impossible to seize opportunities that were sitting on the table. Opportunities that could enable us, finally, to focus on what we love.

Noa Keinan

"I have all kinds of fragments of thoughts. Maybe they'll coalesce into something coherent. Maybe not."

Noa Keinan told me this at the start of our conversation, almost as a warning. She has always been drawn to fragmented writing, she said. But this was something different. The fragmentation was not a style. It was the condition she was living in.

"The basic Israeli Jewish human experience I had after October 7th was a moment of the ground falling away. A loss of the coordinates that define me in the world, in Israeli society. A shock that invaded so many spaces. It reached the level of identity, gender roles at home, the experience of parenthood. And so many thoughts about my grandparents, and how they still, after the Holocaust, remained people who believe in humanity."

Noa grew up in Jerusalem, in Hashomer Hatzair, the socialist Zionist youth movement I grew up in too, one that she says instilled in her, from a young age, an ethos she can still recite without thinking.

"There's no reason to live, no point in living, unless you're fighting."

Not fighting in the military sense, fighting in the civic sense. The political sense. Fighting for what you believe in. For justice. For a better world, which is possible, which is so close, one that we can create together. What we used to call 'swimming against the stream.'

She carries this with her even today, into her work to strengthen local government, working for a major foundation in Israel. Her husband works at Maoz, an organization that builds leadership for Israeli civil society. They are raising children on a kibbutz. Everything about her life is organized around the proposition that you can change the world through action. Through building systems, training leaders, doing the work.

And then the coordinates that defined her place in the world vanished.

I asked Noa what occupied her most in the months after October 7th. She told me it was not the war itself, not the military analysis or the political crisis, though those were present. It was something else.

"The central thing that occupied me, consciously, was trying to understand this event of the global Left. Their perception of us. Of our friends. How people who believe in the same things, the same values, can flip on us so quickly."

She described it with an image that had stayed with her.

"How can it be that you meet an Iranian in Europe and you say, 'Wow, it must be so hard to be Iranian, how difficult with that government of yours,' but when you are the Israeli abroad, those same people who share your values see you only as the occupier? That stunned me."

She told me about her sister, who had been living in the United States for five years, studying at Yale and then doing a residency in Maine. More than a year after October 7th, someone at the residency asked her: "How is your family?" Her sister was shocked. It was the first time anyone had asked. In over a year.

"She was in a writing course. She read something – nothing to do with politics – and the students told her: everything you say is from the perspective of the occupier. The professor said nothing. No support. She just stopped going to that class."

Noa paused.

"Dismissal. That's what she experienced. Dismissal. And I hear it from every direction."

She put aside the political analysis, the war that began as justified and became, as she put it, the fulfillment of this government's darkest fantasies. Enough said about that, she told me. What she could not put aside was the feeling of alienation.

"It introduced me to a different type of emotion. A different type of fear. Not the same kind of fear I've felt in any other situation."

She told me about an experience years earlier, on a bus in Germany. She was on a youth movement delegation. One of her group was wearing a Falcon movement shirt, the German social-democratic youth. A skinhead got on the bus in Hanover and did the Nazi salute. It wasn't aimed at them specifically. He had seen the Falcon shirt, the antifa symbol.

"But I remember the feeling. Something aimed at my very existence. Very strange. Very, very strange."

She looked at me.

"This feeling of alienation from people I used to know is similar. It doesn't matter what my positions are, what my actions are. It's my very existence they object to. That's the thing."

I asked Noa how her relationship with Israel – not the state practically, but the idea of the state – had changed.

She tried to answer, then stopped herself. She told me she struggled now to even remember how she had felt before. There was a trend on Instagram, she told me, people posting photos from 2016, a kind of nostalgia for the world before COVID, before the wars, before everything.

"I genuinely struggle to remember the mindset. But I think that in the essential, fundamental sense, my Zionism, my understanding of the struggle over the direction of Zionism, I don't think anything dramatic changed. We were already in a very different place. Bibi was already prime minister. It's been clear for a long time that there's a battle over Zionism, and it's become more and more clear that we've lost it."

"I will say I've become much more of a small-believer in the ability of things to change. But maybe I was always a small-believer. Because I think the specific weight of positive potential in what we do here has been very small for the past few decades."

That felt to me like a contradiction in terms. A believer in the ability to change, but only a little, only on the margins, while things were going from bad to worse. So I asked her the question I knew so many of my friends were asking themselves: given things are bad, and you believe they can only change a little, not a lot, do you intend to keep raising your children here?

"Yes. What am I going to do?"

She almost laughed.

"I grew up in Hashomer Hatzair. There's no reason to live, no point in living, unless you're fighting. That ethos is embedded in me from a young age. Deeply. The thought didn't come up – not living here. It's not an option."

I pressed her, though, because I too know people who grew up with an activist ethos who have chosen to go the other way. What is the root of the decision to stay and fight?

"It's not rational," she said. "It's connected to language, in its mental sense. Not the technical. It's who I am. I understand the world through the coordinates of the Zionist project in Israel. It's literally in my DNA."

Her answer made me want to better understand what she thought about the choice parents make to raise children in Israel, in a world that has isolated Israel, one that declared Israel to be antithetical to the world order it seeks to keep. How can we raise a generation with her internal strength, her commitment to fighting the hard, nearly intractable yet existentially necessary fights?

She paused.

"We are a society with a mental disorder. A severe mental disorder," she answered. There seems to be a disconnect between cause and effect that has become the defining condition of the age. People post their narratives on social media and nothing connects to anything. Citizens vote and nothing changes. Actions have no discernible consequences. "And that's the most dangerous thing. Because when people feel that nothing they do matters, they stop doing anything. Or worse – they stop caring what they do."

This is why Noa believes it is so important to focus our efforts on local politics. Because civil society proved time and again to be able to make the small changes that had a huge effect on peoples' everyday lives. Local action most clearly connects cause and effect, needs and actions.

By building on the local, Noa believes, we can build up towards actual change. It won't be easy. It will take time. But it can happen, if we focus on changing institutions close to home and then building on those institutions to make larger changes. Because the challenge is grand, and the days are short. "We need to build public service. Build capabilities. Build differently, in a way that gives much more room to local government. We need to rehabilitate the north, rehabilitate the south. Rehabilitate civic trust. Rehabilitate the social fabric. Rehabilitate education. Rehabilitate the youth movements. There's so much to rehabilitate."

One of the organizations she believes is pioneering this type of local-to-national work is the Social Justice Centers (Tzedek Centers). "What's powerful in what they do is that despite the work being Sisyphean, it's daily. It's organized in a certain way, and it manages to make you feel that there is value. That there is a connection between cause and effect. That there is value to the action I take. And then suddenly I understand: my actions can have value. I can influence reality."

That, for her, was what made them special.

"That's mind-blowing in today's world. In a world so disconnected – where it doesn't matter what you do – this thing restores the connection. Between what you do and what happens."

She told me this was the same thing that happens in youth movements, the same thing that had shaped her childhood and her path to political and social involvement. The feeling that you belong to something, that your actions matter, that there is a link between what you do and what changes.

"It's a sense of civic agency. That's exactly what happens in a youth movement. But if it doesn't happen at scale, it loses its power. The depth and the scale, when they come together. I see something unique in that."

She paused.

"And it happens through legwork. Through the daily work on the ground. Not through narratives. Not through slogans. Through showing up."

This is the model she believes will help Israel rebuild itself, piece by piece, and in doing so repair the connection between action and consequence that the modern world has severed.

"Every one of these efforts is fragile. Every little flame can be extinguished at any moment. The fact that it exists at all is a miracle. The fact that it exists under this government is a miracle."

As our conversation came to a close, I asked Noa what she thought could rebuild the Israeli spirit. Not politically, but at the level of the human experience.

"We need to amplify the spirit," she said. "We need to give space and promote and fund through the state higher education, the humanities, the arts. Which is the exact opposite of everything we're doing as a state."

She described art the way someone describes oxygen.

"The highest role of art is to open a crack in the existing order of life. To allow you, for a moment, to step outside the existing order of life through a great work of art, to be enveloped by it. And then to return to your life, but with that potential inside you."

She told me her favorite book in the world is *The World of Yesterday* by Stefan Zweig. I told her it was mine, too. Zweig was a popular writer in the German language during the *Fin de Siècle*, the turn of the 20th century. Austrian at birth, Zweig wrote often that he felt at home in the German language, much like Noa said her home was in Hebrew. This feeling of belonging to German connected him with other writers, poets, playwrights across Europe working in the German language and beyond it. One of them being Theodor Herzl, one of the German language's brightest stars of the period, editor of the Neue Freie Presse, and an essayist, cultural critic, and playwright himself.

Zweig was not convinced by Herzl's vision and did not join the Zionist movement. He continued feeling at home in the German language up until the moment the German people burned his books and forced him into exile in 1934. He documented this experience – the rise and fall of Jewish acceptance into humanist Europe, the rise and fall of the Jewish Golden Age in the German Language – in his final book, *The World of Yesterday*, which he finished just before taking his own life in Petropolis, near Rio de Janeiro, on the other side of the world from his beloved home.

I've long recommended people to read the book because of how poignantly it describes our present. How the same dynamics of acceptance and rejection, how the same desire for assimilation and acceptance often leads to the equal and opposite reaction by the nations Jews have, historically, sought to join. It is a heartbreaking, beautiful portrait of some of the most important writers and thinkers in modern European history, and in its avoidance of Zionism it makes the strongest case I can imagine for the relevance of its core idea.

For Noa, however, it explains her feeling of alienation from the world she knew. Her feeling of exile from the global, humanist Left. "He distills exactly that. I identify with it at different points in my life, at deep levels. What existed has ceased to exist. That is the grief. A grief of humanity, a grief of the spirit, a grief of everything."

Zweig and his wife, Lotte, killed themselves in 1942. If he had lived three more years, he would have seen the fall of Nazi Germany. Six more and he would have seen the establishment of the State of Israel. Forty more and he would have lived to see the unification of Europe born out of the ashes of its destruction – the fulfillment of the very dream he had spent his life articulating. I think of that often, when the days are darkest. How time has the habit of making previously assumed trends an artifact of the past.

Which is why we need to prepare the grounds for a better future instead of lamenting the troubles of the present. Which is why Noa believes in small actions, even those which seem like they may not add up to much on the national or international scale.

"I'm not a writer. I'm not an intellectual. I'm not an artist. That's not my role in the world. My role is to act. That's the dialogue between two parallel axes: the world of action and the world of spirit, of human experience. They're parallel. They're another tension." Each of us has our role to play, none of us have the excuse not to play it.

What stays with me from my conversation with Noa is the honesty with which she expresses the fragmentation she is experiencing, and her commitment to the whole nonetheless. She did not pretend to have a vision. She did not offer an overarching program. Despite the coordinates of her life being lost, despite feeling that the existing order had ceased to exist, she knows a new order will soon be born. She accepts she is living in the space between.

And that is why she is still here. Not because it makes sense, necessarily. She told me twice that sometimes she thinks it doesn't, that rationally it's stupid to remain committed to a project beset by so many adversaries. Yet here she remains, committed. Because it's in her DNA. Because Hashomer Hatzair taught her that life without struggling for a better world has no meaning. Because the Hebrew language, in its deepest sense, is how she understands the world.

Despite the fragments, despite the difficulty, despite moments of despair, Noa holds onto the fragments of the Israel she loves, knowing they may never coalesce. Her commitment is to go on building anyway. Not a grand project. Not a national narrative. Local. As a daily practice. A perhaps Sisyphean act of showing up – in a municipal office, in a social justice center, in a youth movement – aimed at restoring, piece by piece, the severed connection between what you do and what happens. In the only place she feels at home. Because the alternative, as Zweig showed, is to stop living altogether.

And that, for Noa Keinan, is not an option.

Mike Berman

On October 6th, 2023, Michael ("Mike") Berman was in Boston at the wedding of his best friend's daughter. He woke up on the morning of October 7th to a text message from his wife: "call me." He called her just before seeing the headlines. By the time he woke up the attack was already seven hours old, and it was clear his world had changed. "By the time I woke up in Boston, it was clear that this was the beginning of a war and that the world was going to change dramatically for an awful lot of people."

I met Mike years ago through a friend and colleague in the medical diagnostics company I cofounded, MobileODT. Mike is a pillar of the Israeli medtech community, one of the few people in Israel who has built and sold medical device companies to global corporations headquartered in Europe and the United States, who maintains vast networks within those corporations, and who now invests across the medical spectrum. Over the years Mike became a mentor whose advice I came to deeply value, and I was surprised to run into him in the lobby of a Haaretz conference in the midst of the war. It was there I learned that Mike's politics are similar to mine: proudly liberal, democratic, born of the Left, somewhat homeless in the current moment. Mike shared with me that he is getting more involved in supporting civil causes and in his political activism. I asked him if he would talk about it, and he agreed.

I wanted to feature Mike's perspective because he has seen Israel from more angles than most people I know. He is the quintessential insider-outsider, a person who got to know Israel once he was already old enough to think critically about it, an adult who learned about how it is to grow up in Israel through his children, a professional who had businesses to run despite the wars and bans and boycotts, an Israeli father with a child abroad. Mike has experienced Israel's reputation rise and fall and his engagement with politics ebb and flow over the years. He has been a consistently critical voice against the Netanyahu government. He and his wife were out nearly every Saturday night in 2023, demonstrating to defend Israeli democracy during the judicial crisis.

And yet Mike is not an ideologue. He describes himself as someone who has held "a very realistic and sober view of Zionism" since he was young, and thinks of himself as an idealist and a realist at the same time.

"I remember when I was eighteen years old, I spent a weekend up in Upper Nazareth, being hosted by a family up there and just being integrated for a long weekend into their life. And seeing, wow, this was not the ideological Zionism that I grew up with in upstate New York. This was much more raw."

Define raw? I asked.

"I got exposed to the fissures between Mizrahim and Ashkanazim, the divisions with Arab Israelis...since then I never had a naive ideological view that suddenly came crashing down on the rocks. I've been an idealist and a realist all at the same time for many, many years. So, for me, I always felt that what we have been experiencing was just a continuation of those stress and strain points in Israeli society, both the judicial coup as well as everything that came out from the war with Hamas."

It was his idealist side, I'm assuming, that assured Mike on October 7th that "the army will clean this up real fast." And then, as the hours passed, his realist side kicked in. He realized the army was not cleaning it up, and was not able to respond in the way he had expected.

"It dragged on. Partly because of the scope of the attack, literally thousands of Hamas fighters crossing the border. And the army was clearly being taken by surprise. They were not prepared for this. And that became apparent very, very quickly."

He was in Boston, his family in Israel, trying to make sense of information that arrived faster than anyone could process it. As the scale of the violence became apparent to Mike, and as reports kept fragmenting and contradicting each other, an image formed in its head, a historical example he used to explain what was happening to himself: "Once again, these Jews were slaughtered like they were in Kishinev, like they were in

Hebron in 1929, like they have been throughout Jewish history."

While I had heard Kishinev evoked before in reference to October 7th, I had not yet heard anyone compare Hamas' attack to the massacres of Jews which began in Hebron in 1929. That reference struck a personal chord, because I spent much of my senior year at Columbia working on an honors thesis in political economy that focused on what were then called the Hebron Riots.

My thesis, *From Brother to Other*, sought to understand how relations between Jews and Arabs could deteriorate so thoroughly – leading to neighbor attacking neighbor in the city that had, until that point, been a symbol of coexistence, called Al Khalil, or The Friend in Arabic. I had suggested that the enmity came from imposed resource constriction due to British mismanagement, a possibly unintentional 'divide and conquer' effect that caused liberation movements that formerly saw in each other a potential source of support to turn on each other in the hope of gaining advantage. In other words, I sought to make the case for coexistence and to counter the arguments that the Zionist movement and the movement for Arab self-determination were inherently contradictory. I argued that the Hebron riots were directed by external forces who sought to sow division between neighbors to gain advantage – and use that as the basis for arguing how we can respond to such foreign meddling maintaining enmity today.

When Mike mentioned Hebron it coalesced something for me: I've come to believe that Hamas' attacks should not be seen as an inherently Palestinian action but rather as an attempt by a coalition of actors – funded primarily by Iran, probably with Qatari support – to sabotage normalization between the Jewish State and the Muslim World. (It is sometimes hard to remember that the same Benjamin Netanyahu who ordered the destruction of Gaza was on the floor of the UN in September 2023, sharing with the world his commitment to a historic agreement he worked towards with Saudi Arabia's Crown Prince Mohammed bin Salman).

Given that historical analogy, and its implications on where the responsibility lies, I asked him what he thought Israel's response should be, his gut reaction in those first hours.

"Immediate gut reaction was that Israel needed to unite and react strongly and do everything in its power to prevent something like this from ever happening again." And he understood the implications. "Already on the first day, I knew that this was going to be a disaster for Gaza. I just couldn't imagine a situation where Gaza wasn't going to be devastated as a result of what the Gazans and the Gazan government did."

He reminded me of the statement made on day one by Yoav Gallant (who was then Israel's Minister of Defense), that in past conflicts with Hamas the political echelon had always stopped the defense establishment, calling them back each time. Encounter and pull back. Encounter and pull back. This time, Gallant said, that was not going to be the case.

"I think it was very clear from day one that this was going to be a different kind of war with Hamas. I don't think anybody expected it would last for two years. I certainly didn't. I was thinking about it in terms of months. And I was pretty convinced that there was going to be terrible devastation in Gaza with a lot of loss of life and a lot of loss of innocent life. So it all came crashing in real quick to me that this was the direction we were going."

Given his immediate reaction, and what he's seen play out since, I asked Mike whether he felt the response got out of control.

"Absolutely. It got out of control because of the policies pursued by the prime minister and the government, where they had their own political interests much more in mind than they did the interest of Israel and the Israeli public. I don't think that was the case as much at the beginning of the war as it was six, twelve, eighteen months into it."

And here Mike makes an important distinction I heard quite a few times from people who fought or whose loved ones fought in the war: while the primary responsibility for the destruction of Gaza lay with those who lay traps under the houses and hospitals of innocents, Israel definitely had its share of responsibility to take. Most of the responsibility lay on the political level, certainly, but we cannot ignore the fact that the command level in the military behaved irresponsibly as a means of placating those same political leaders who let the disaster happen on their watch.

"One of the first things the Israeli military did was change the rules of engagement. So instead of needing a colonel or a general in order to open fire, it was like the lowliest private or sergeant, they saw anything suspicious and basically anything that moved got shot."

This was a decision made by the military leadership, not an accident, and it led to unprecedented death and maiming of the Gazan population. Mike does not believe its aim was to harm civilians (and neither do I, after quite a few interviews and a lot of research) but I believe it is important to separate intention and consequence when it comes to human life. Even if the military's intention was to protect its soldiers from attackers popping out of the intricate tunnel system developed by Hamas over the past decades, its consequences were tragic. Perhaps even criminal.

"I don't think that there were – best I can tell – too many examples of war crimes. But there probably were some war crimes. I do not believe that there was genocide by any rational definition of what genocide is. But it was a pretty ugly war. And there were an awful lot of innocent civilians who were killed and injured and suffering. The group primarily responsible for that, in my eyes, is Hamas. I think that the Israeli government made a bunch of bad decisions along the way that exacerbated a bad situation and made it quite a bit worse."

I pressed him on the trade-off, the question that haunts every conversation about this war. Why prioritize the safety of

Israeli soldiers over innocent Palestinian civilians? Despite making clear that he values every human life, he did not flinch in explaining that he feels there is, when it comes down to it, a reality we need to recognize.

"There are a lot of things in life that are unfair. Most things in life are unfair. And I hate to sound callous, but in war there are winners and losers. I don't have any problem with the Israel Defense Forces prioritizing the safety of its soldiers. If the consequence of that is that there will be more innocent civilians killed, then that's a trade-off that I personally am willing to accept."

"Would I have preferred that the Israel Air Force didn't need to be as active as they were in taking out targets, which of course is going to cause much more collateral damage? I would have preferred that. But I think that probably would have put a lot more Israeli soldiers at risk. Instead of having hundreds that were killed, there would have been thousands."

He shook his head.

"There's nothing easy here. It's messy. It's not easy. This is what happens in war."

Which is why, I responded, we need to do our utmost to avoid war in the first place.

As the war ground on, Mike watched Israeli society fracture and recombine into a new set of civil forces. He described his experience observing the landscape of protest that emerged in the months after October 7th, and the competing gatherings that mapped the fault lines of Israeli civic life in the days after the attacks, after the rocket alert sirens stopped or at least were down to a minimum, when people could head out into the streets again.

"There were the people that came to the hostage square to support the hostage families. And then a kilometer away on Kaplan Street, there were people that would get together to protest the conduct of the government." He shared that a friend described it as, "the sad protest, the mad protest, and then afterwards, at the Begin Bridge, there was the sad-mad protest. So you had it all."

Mike and his wife were among the first in their circle to get back out on the streets after the attacks to protest the government's decisions and the conduct of the war months before many of their friends felt it was appropriate.

"I had quite a number of friends who were not willing to go out in protest against government actions, whereas my wife and I were ready to do that and did that quite a bit earlier."

He shared with me the competing thoughts that ran through his head during those months – thoughts that every Israeli I knew struggled with: do you protest in support of the hostages given how poorly the government was running their recovery, or would that just help Hamas by raising the ante? Do you protest to have the government take responsibility for falling asleep on their shift in the hope of their resignation, or do you stay off the streets in order to give them the space to do their jobs? Many people I knew felt it was complicated – and Mike felt that in spades in his community, and with himself.

"I remember early on thinking, it might make sense for the hostage families just to keep their heads low. Because the more they protest in favor of the hostages, ironically, that could actually increase the price that Hamas wants to exact out of the government, which could reduce the chances of getting a deal done. That was a fairly rational thought, but a fleeting one. We just went with our human instinct, which was to support the hostage families. Just have to support them in their pain and in their struggle."

I interviewed Mike once the war with Gaza was "over," according to Donald Trump: Israel occupied a wide strip of land within Gaza, with Israeli troops on the Israeli side and Hamas ruling with an iron fist on the other. Given the outcome of the war, I asked Mike what he hopes we as a country, as a people, learn from the destruction of Gaza. He answered with the directness I had come to expect from him.

"I hope that there's learning on both sides." Israel, he hopes, will learn that "You can defend yourself with military force, but at the end you need to have some sort of a non-military mechanism for coming to an arrangement with your neighbors. There is no full military solution for this." Which is what so deeply infuriated him about the conduct of the government, that they forgot the lessons learned in blood by previous generations, that force is but a tool to work towards peace. "Military force and always extending the olive branch. Always have the olive branch." He said it twice, as if to make sure I had heard it. "I don't think this government has done that at all. It's been all military force and no extending of an olive branch."

Netanyahu's government did the opposite. It delayed any talk of an olive branch so long as it included a conversation with or about the Palestinians.

"I think it's been a terrible policy of Netanyahu for the last two decades to try to disempower the Palestinian Authority. I think it would have been much smarter to try to help reform and empower the Palestinian Authority. And that's how we ended up where we are today."

I asked him what he meant.

"It's this concept that we will empower Hamas, split the Palestinian leadership, help encourage the split so that we can say, 'Hey, there's no partner to negotiate with.' What kind of leadership is that? That's destructive, that's not constructive."

This was, he made the case, similar to Golda Meir's failure to take Egyptian overtures seriously in the early 1970s. A template for what not to do.

"There's this mentality: when you're weak, you can't negotiate with the enemy. And when you're powerful, you don't have to negotiate with the enemy. And I would hope that the leadership of Israel has a balanced approach, emphasizing military defense and military capabilities and at the same time constantly pushing for finding ways of compromising to resolve conflicts."

And the lesson he hopes the Palestinians internalize?

"They can't win," can't defeat Israel militarily, won't drive the Jews into the sea. There will be no Greater Palestine for them. "They are going to have to compromise. And it pains me to say it, but for generations now, the majority of Palestinians have been uncompromising in their view. The Palestinian leadership was offered multiple times, starting in the 1930s, compromises. And they have been very consistent in rejecting those compromises all the way through."

He took a second to find the words.

"I pity them. I pity the Palestinian population who's had the leadership that they've had. Just as much as I'm angry at the Israeli leadership that I've had."

When I asked Mike how he distinguished between the state and the government, between Zionism and the people currently in power operating in its name, he told me he had been wrestling with this question since he was a teenager.

"There was always an idealistic element to Zionism. There was always a bit of a utopian element: to change the fate of the Jewish people and to have a homeland." He sees the country at a crossroads. Two paths.

"One direction is the messianic right, along with the non-Zionist ultra-Orthodox, essentially continuing to control the levers of power and moving the country inexorably in the direction of their vision. Which is ultra-nationalism and racism and exemption of the ultra-Orthodox from really being participants and members of Israeli society in any meaningful way. Just continuing to suck resources from the working secular public."

He was blunt about what that would mean for him personally.

"If the battle is won by the Kahanists," he said, using the term for the extreme Right followers of the late Rabbi Meir Kahane, "that would be a crisis for me personally in my Zionism."

The other path, he said, is possible, maybe even probable.

"In the upcoming elections, I think it's very possible that the parties currently in opposition will in some form take over. That they will start dismantling many of the Kahanist and extreme messianist policies. They will remove some of the financial subsidies on the ultra-Orthodox population."

He pointed to a precedent. Years ago when Yair Lapid served as finance minister, the removal of subsidies led to measurable increases in ultra-Orthodox employment within two years. A population who swore to remain the same for eternity started to send more of its members into the workforce, empower women to take higher paying jobs, reduced their birth rate to compensate.

"These incentives do matter. And there's a lot more fluidity than I think people appreciate in movements between religious and non-religious, ultra-Orthodox and Orthodox. It's not this static situation."

"It could go one way or the other. I know which direction I'm going to push in my own little world, which is to have a liberal, democratic, progressive Jewish country that's not messianist and not Kahanist, where we share the burden. But it's going to be a dicey next decade, that's for sure."

As our conversation was wrapping up, I asked Mike about something that had been nagging me: how the Jewish world outside Israel was processing this, and whether American Jews in particular were equipped to hold the complexity we were experiencing in Israel, as liberals, democrats, Zionists.

"The Jewish people is one big dysfunctional family," he said. "And it's always the question of: do I support, do I not support? And it all boils down to: if it's a member of your family, you do what you got to do. You support and you love. It doesn't mean you don't criticize. It doesn't mean you solve all the dysfunction."

But the dysfunction, he said, runs deep, and it starts with how American Jews have built their institutions.

"A lot of the biggest American Jewish organizations have really weakened because they were trying to be things for all Jews. They've sort of gone to the lowest common denominator, which has resulted in organizations that aren't very compelling for anybody."

And then he turned to something that clearly had been bothering him for a long time.

"I think that tikkun olam has been sort of fetishized as the supreme Jewish value. And I have no problem with tikkun olam. I think it's a wonderful Jewish value. But it's gotten to the point where people look at it as something where it really is—it's almost being used as a weapon. As kind of an ideological purity test. Are you in favor of tikkun olam? Well, then you have to be in favor of X, and you have to be against Y."

He shook his head.

"That's not how the world works. That's not how Jewish values work. There are many Jewish values, it's not just tikkun olam. There's also the value of the defense of the Jewish people, which is a tremendous Jewish value. And the establishment of a home for the Jewish people. These things need to be held in balance."

He connected this directly to what he was watching happen in the American Jewish community after October 7th.

"If you've reduced your Judaism to one supreme value – social justice, tikkun olam – and then somebody tells you that Israel is committing genocide, you're stuck. You can't support Israel. You have no framework for it. Your one value says: this is wrong, full stop. There's no room for complexity."

"But if you understand that being Jewish involves a basket of values, that self-defense is a Jewish value, that building a homeland is a Jewish value, that caring for the stranger is a Jewish value, and that these sometimes conflict with each other, then you can hold the tension. You can say: this war is ugly, and it may also be necessary. You can mourn Palestinian deaths and still believe in the right of your army to fight. The purity test doesn't let you do that. The basket does."

He told me he had watched this play out in his own circles, friends and family members in America who could not engage with what Israel was going through because their framework had no room for such complexity.

"They just shut down. They can't talk about it. They've got one lens and it doesn't fit, so they either condemn Israel entirely or they go silent. And that's a failure. Not of morality, but of Jewish education. We raised a generation on a single value and then were surprised when they couldn't hold complexity."

I asked him why he thought outsiders, Jews and non-Jews, struggle so much with Israel's complexity. He leaned back and thought about it.

"We live here and we see all the different colors of the rainbow. We see the complexity, the textures, the sounds and smells. It's a very real world for us. For the average American Jew, even the average engaged American Jew, there's a lot of that detail that's missing. They're just looking for a big narrative, a big theme. Israel good. Israel bad. Zionism good. Zionism bad. It has to fit into a pretty general bucket."

It is that distance, he believes, that flattens out the complexity, leading people to fit Israel into one of their pre-determined buckets.

"Why is it that there's so much resonance for the Palestinian cause in Western democracies? I think a lot of it boils down to: there's the powerful one and the weak one. Israel is the powerful one. The Palestinians are the weak one. The natural reaction for most people and most governments is, hey, the powerful one should back off. And guess what? We're the same way."

He gave me an example.

"When you read about some conflict in Bosnia or Sudan, like me, you know very, very little about what's really going on there. The background, the history, who's right and who's wrong. My initial reaction is, hey, the powerful guys should back off. Let the weak guys breathe. But I don't really know much about Sudan or Bosnia or Somaliland. What the hell do I really know about that? I really don't know very much. But it doesn't stop me from having an opinion."

He laughed.

"I spent as much time thinking about the Bosnian conflict as I do trying to decide which peanut butter to buy."

The laughter faded.

"And I think it's the same way for most people in the world, including Jews outside of Israel. They're informed, but they don't really understand the complexities."

He shared with me a bit about a recent conversation with his brother, when Mike had been trying to explain the situation, and kept saying, as he always does: it's complicated.

"At one point my brother said to me, 'It's not complicated.' And I said, 'Well, that's your view.' But that's the gap. If you're here, you know it's complicated. If you're not here, you want it to be simple. And it just isn't."

When I asked Mike, finally, whether he was optimistic, he gave me the answer I should have expected from someone who has called himself an idealist and a realist since he was eighteen.

"I don't use the word optimistic. I use the word hopeful. I'm hopeful. I think there's a path forward. I think it's narrow. I think it requires leadership that we don't currently have. I think it requires a public that is willing to compromise on things that are really hard to compromise on."

He paused.

"And I think it requires the rest of the world to understand that this is complicated. That we're not the bad guys and we're not the good guys. We're people, trying to build something, in a really tough neighborhood, with a really flawed government, doing the best we can."

He smiled. A tired smile. One I've seen again and again on people holding that complexity, trying to convince loved ones that they are not the bad guy, patient to the best of their ability.

"It's not like I had some naive ideological view. I never did. But I'll tell you what: I still believe in the project. I believe in the project of a liberal, democratic, Jewish homeland. I just think we have a lot of work to do to get there. And I'm not going anywhere."

He told me he sometimes catches himself thinking about that weekend in Upper Nazareth, when he was eighteen. The Mizrahi family who hosted him, the fissures he saw for the first time, the gap between the Zionism he'd learned in upstate New York and the country he was actually standing in.

"I remember thinking even then: okay, this is harder than they told me. But it's real. And real is better than pretty."

He laughed again.

"I still think that. Real is better than pretty. This place is real. Messy, frustrating, infuriating, beautiful. And real. And that's enough for me."

Michal Sherez Shilor

Michal Sherez Shilor tells me she has a history of changing her mind. She grew up in what she calls "your regular typical liberal American Jewish home. Conservative synagogue that you drive to on Shabbat, that kind of thing." Her activism started young: against bullying in school, for LGBTQ+ rights, what she described as a basic sense of tzedek, of justice, that she followed intuitively wherever it led. She moved to Israel with Garin Tzabar (an organization that helps young adults immigrate together to Israel with the Israel Scouts movement), and she went on to serve in the army, and then travel the world as many Israelis do after their military service.

It was in South Africa that she found herself in conversations where people talked about Israel through the lens of their own history, as apartheid, colonialism, occupation. It was there and then that she came to feel that she did not understand the situation in her own country well enough to respond.

"I came back to Israel with an agenda of learning about the conflict here before I do anything else in the world."

So she joined an Arab-Jewish dialogue facilitation training once she returned and, for the first time, met Arab citizens of Israel. Not Palestinians in the West Bank, but Israeli citizens, who told her that when they were young, they had dreams of the Israeli army destroying their homes.

"That was a shock to me. Because how could that be? The Israeli army is the most humane army in the world. Right?"

As a result of that she went to Jerusalem, to learn about East Jerusalem by walking through it, talking to people, and listening to how life was actually lived on the other side of the city most Jewish Israelis never visited.

"That sent me to the very radical left. So for a couple of years, I found myself every Friday in Sheikh Jarrah or protesting against Israeli settlements. I lost friends who didn't want to talk to me anymore because all I was interested in was talking about the human rights crisis in East Jerusalem."

But Michal, being Michal, continued to question her own positions. After working at the Jerusalem Intercultural Center for a while she began asking herself whether any of her activism was making a difference.

"Are these solidarity protests on Fridays effective? What are we doing here? What are we doing? I am standing in solidarity with my Palestinian neighbors. So they know that not all Jews are what they think. But it's not changing the situation. It's not like I'm affecting anybody, any policymakers or nobody's listening to us. And even more than that, we're just making people even more antagonistic towards us."

Asking herself that question on effectiveness changed the trajectory of her life. She began what she called a gradual movement toward a different kind of activism, a different type of politics, one she still struggles to name.

"You could call it the center, but it's not really the center. It's just a place that tries to be effective and practical. I have this ideology and I do believe in equal rights and I do believe in all this stuff. But I understand that I can't fully live that ideology from zero to a hundred. At the same time, I have to see what's practical."

I asked her if she'd be willing to share more about her ideology, given how deeply I noticed she held it. She didn't want to.

"I got blinded by this ideology. And all I wanted to do was a hundred percent ideology. But that's not effective. It makes things worse a lot of times."

Jerusalem became her laboratory, where she explored new ways of working, new ways to be effective. She discovered that in a city where people actually live alongside each other – Jews and Arabs, secular and religious, left and right – there was more common ground than the national conversation suggested.

"Jerusalem is a great field for that. Because both the left wing and the right wing, for example, don't necessarily want two Jerusalems. Almost everybody wants one Jerusalem. And that's interesting because your non-Jerusalemite extreme left-wing Israelis want two Jerusalems, but they don't understand what that means. There's something about living in Jerusalem that the complexity can allow you to hold an ideology and translate it in different ways to practical steps."

The project that captured this perfectly for Michal was A Different Day in Jerusalem: *Yom Yerushalmi: Yom HaAcher*. It was founded in response to Jerusalem Day, the annual commemoration of the city's reunification in 1967, when the Israeli military captured it from the Jordanian forces who had occupied it since their conquest of the land in 1948.

In today's Israel, Jerusalem Day is defined by the Flag Parade, a march through the Old City's Muslim Quarter organized by the most radical religious schools and seminaries in Judea and Samaria, and known for its racist and violent dimensions. For most West Jerusalemites, it is not much of a celebration because, as Michal put it, seventy percent of Jerusalemites sit in their homes and wait for the chaos to be over after buses from outside the city bring people in to do their *balagan* (the chaos of the demonstrations and protests of the day can be terrifying). For years she had protested against the Flag Parade. But then she made a shift.

"I organized something called A Different Day in Jerusalem, which brought together activists who want to mark this day in a different way than the Flag Parade. Some people really do want to celebrate the fact that East Jerusalem is unified with West Jerusalem. Even if I don't necessarily want to celebrate that, some people do, and they want to do it in a non-racist way. So why not let them do that? Holding that complexity of how can I make space for somebody who doesn't necessarily want to be racist but does want to celebrate this day."

The event became a tradition, several years running, eighty events within twenty-four hours across the city. She saw it as proof that the approach worked.

"That's a good example of moving from a place of being just against, without any effective anything, to something that became a tradition and really created a different energy in the city."

On October 6th, 2023, Michal was in a complicated place. The judicial reform crisis had left her feeling hopeless. She remembered the night the then Defense Minister Gallant was fired (for the first time), sitting at home, unable to move. She had not gone to many of the mass protests because she had young children and was afraid of police violence. But at one of the larger demonstrations in Jerusalem, she found a small group of rabbis on a hunger strike, and something broke open in her.

"I don't want to fight with the energy that I'm fighting against. I'm fighting against the energy of anger and chaos and destruction. And I don't want to use anger and chaos and destruction to fight that. I want to do something different that breaks this paradigm of two sides coming and meeting in the war zone, and whoever kills the most wins."

She wept.

"I'm crying about the judicial reform. I'm crying about the rift that it's creating. And I want to break out of this bubble that we've been put in and find a different solution."

And then came the morning of October 7th.

"I woke up and told my husband that there's a war. And he said, there's always something. You're always saying it's a war. I said, no, no, listen, this is going to be something big."

Five hours later, Boaz, her husband, got his call-up and left. Michal was in the Golan Heights – they had moved there two months earlier, five kilometers from Syria. Boaz's entire family was visiting for Sukkot, so after he left, she was alone with the children and his family. She was simultaneously WhatsApping with a close friend locked in a safe room in the south with a four-month-old and a three-year-old.

"And as I was chatting with my friend and thinking, what are we doing this close to Syria, what's going to happen? I also realized with my professional side that what I have to do now is to start working to prevent violence inside of Israel, the way it happened in May 2021."

By this point Michal was running the Mixed Cities Department of the Tzedek Centers (the Social Justice Centers), a network of grassroots social justice centers across Israel that work with Jewish and Arab communities. By the evening of October 7th, only thirteen hours after the attack began, she held an emergency Zoom for activists and organizations working in the field known as "shared society," what once was called coexistence.

Two hundred people joined. As soon as the call ended, Boaz's family told her there were rumors that UNIFIL (the United Nations Interim Force in Lebanon) had left their stations in Lebanon. They drove her and the children to Jerusalem that night.

She wandered Jerusalem with her kids for a week, working from wherever she could, whenever she could, parenting alone while organizing the internal front. She hired a staff member three weeks into the war to run a two-million-shekel project. Work was her refuge.

"Everything that was professional, everything that had to do with Arab-Jewish stuff inside of Israel, I was so clear on. I knew exactly what I needed to do, who I needed to bring to the table. So clear. In the morning I was very clear on how to get my kids to school and how to work. And then at night I cried in bed every night, basically."

Boaz served two hundred of the first three hundred days of the war on the northern border, not in Gaza, but part of this war nonetheless. Michal is a pacifist. She has a long spiritual practice. She told me she processed the contradiction by understanding their paths as parallel: his calling was to serve, and hers was to hold the shared society together from the inside. She knew he was an ethical person, and she wanted him there – on the warfront – more than someone who might not make the right choice in a terrible moment. But the contradiction did not resolve neatly. It sat inside her alongside everything else.

I asked her if she considered leaving. She did not.

"I could do the easy thing. I have an American passport. My kids have an American passport. But it's not my calling. I have to be here."

"I am Zionist. I want this country to exist as a Jewish democratic state."

As the war continued and reports of casualties and destruction and pain and suffering from Gaza mounted, Michal did not retreat from her commitments. She held questions, more questions than most people I spoke to were willing to hold. Gaza was not an abstraction for her. She knew people whose families were there. She felt their pain. She mourned the destruction of Gaza. Yet throughout it all she kept both things in mind: that what was happening in Gaza was tragic and awful and that she also knew she didn't know the whole story.

"Life is more complicated than saying it's genocide or not. It's more complicated than that. And also life in Gaza is more complicated than saying they're pro or anti the war. You're dealing with a population that is very, very poor, that lives...many of them live on subsidies given by Hamas. Because I have friends and their families that are in Gaza. So it's...I can't...it's not just like a random thing for me."

"I don't know what I would be if I was born in Gaza. I don't know what my thoughts would be. I wouldn't be pro-October 7th. But I'm not sure I would even know the atrocities of October 7th, because I don't think it even streamed everywhere the way that Israel thinks it did."

She told me about a friend, an IDF soldier, who had posted a picture of himself with a V sign, a house burning in the background. She sent him a message telling him she didn't think he should be proud of it. She asked Boaz the same question she was asking herself: how much of what happens in this war looks like that photo, and how much looks like what you do?

"I don't know if we'll ever know the answer to that. Ever."

That led her to draw a line, not between Israel and the world, but between individuals and the collective.

"The individuals that did terrible things in the war will have individual stains on themselves for the rest of their lives. But it's theirs. It's not mine to deal with. I don't think it's an Israeli stain yet."

She believes the silent majority agrees with her. That most Israelis, those who are committed to a liberal, democratic state, a Jewish State, whose Zionism is one of liberation, share her commitment to both living in Israel and acting morally, even in war.

Recognizing that silent majority – the people who do not commit atrocities, on both sides, in Israel as well as in Gaza – is the thing she believes most observers fail to do. We should be highlighting them, strengthening them, making them visible. Instead, entire populations get defined by their worst members, and the majority that wants to live in peace disappears from view.

I asked Michal whether October 7th or the destruction of Gaza by Israel's forces had changed her core beliefs.

"I still believe many of the things that I believed before October 7th. I believe in equal rights. I believe in education. I believe in the field of shared society. I believe in partnership. But I'm more compassionate about how hard it is for each side. I'm more compassionate. I have more compassion towards people that voted for Bibi. I have more compassion for people on both sides that live with a tremendous amount of fear that controls their decision making."

That, to me, was the most Michal thing she said in our entire conversation. A willingness to question herself and her position, an openness to seeing the other side on their terms. A deepening of empathy for the very people she disagrees with.

I asked her what she is trying to save.

"I think I'm trying to save my life. The Israel I know as a sentimental place, as a beautiful place with beautiful nature, with amazing people, with diversity that I love. I love the diversity here. I think it's amazing. There's a lot of hope here. It's a state that symbolizes hope in a lot of senses. And it's what I know. It's sentimental. It's mine. This is the place that I feel like I belong in. I've moved many times in my life and I've never felt at home anywhere except for here."

I asked her what her next steps were, how she believes she could have more impact on Israel and its future. She shared with me that she had gone back and forth for twelve years on whether to run for office herself and always came to the same conclusion: the national system is designed to eat alive people who hold complexity. The Knesset selects for those willing to deal in absolutes.

"We're living in a time of corruption and big money and if you have a pure heart, you cannot get anywhere far."

"That's why the local government I think is a great place to be in. Because it's a lot less influenced by money and big power."

She decided to focus on the local level through her work in the Tzedek (Social Justice) Centers, where she sees change bubbling up from below, especially in Palestinian Israeli society, where a generation is demanding inclusion rather than accepting marginalization. She had already felt the shift In the Arab-Jewish work she had been doing for years: more willingness to step into shared civic spaces, more impatience with the old politics of separatism and victimhood. October 7th accelerated it when the internal fabric held and the violence of May 2021 did not repeat. In the aftermath, new partnerships formed that would have been unthinkable before.

I asked Michal, towards the end of our conversation, whether she was hopeful. She told me she was because she could see the shift happening, people who could not have been in the same room before October 7th now sitting together and saying they had to figure this out. That gave her hope. I asked her if there was anything in particular that gave her hope in those conversations that she could share. "It sounds silly," she replied, "but it's the complexity. It's the fact that things aren't black and white." That people were willing to admit the grey into their conversation, to ease their defenses and accept that "life isn't black and white."

I found hope in Michal's ability to live in the mode of ever questioning, in her openness to change and grow and evolve, to focus on effectiveness and not ideological purity. I was inspired by how she found her answer not in national politics but in the local, the specific, the achievable. Her mindset is, in my opinion, the antidote to people on both sides who are either antizionist or anti-Palestinian. To those who guard their righteousness zealously and do not situate themselves in a wider world where multiple truths could coexist without trumping the other.

Because I've found that Israel, for too many, is either all good or all bad. Either the eternal victim or the eternal aggressor. Either always David or always Goliath. But Israel, like every other country, like every other nation, is neither. It is complicated. It does good things and bad. It has Palestinians who want to integrate into it, and has Palestinians who want to separate from it. It has racists who march through the Arab Quarter once a year waving Israeli flags, and it has liberal democrats who have marched and rallied week after week for years waving that same flag calling for equality and human rights. It has destroyed Gaza, it has waged a war that has killed too many innocents, and it has done so because it was attacked and its people live in fear and they lash out like so many other peoples have lashed out over the course of human history.

That is not to excuse Israel from the violence it wrought. It isn't to justify Israel's decisions after October 7th, blinded by rage and seeking vengeance for its killed, its raped, its wounded, its orphaned. But it is a call to find the space between ideology and life, as Michal did, as she tries to make something beautiful out of what remains. It is a call to be effective in our engagement with Israel, practical with our actions, dedicated to making it a home we are proud of despite its contradictions and challenges.

Bernard Avishai

"I'm speaking with a certain self-critical distance because I haven't had a direct point of suffering from this war over the last three years. So I might come across a little callous, a little cold and analytical. I just want to acknowledge it from the beginning."

Bernard ("Bernie") Avishai wanted the disclaimer on the record, because when I briefed him on what I would like to talk with him about – the Gaza war and its consequences for the foreseeable future – I had checked first to see if it would be too painful for him to discuss. I asked him how it could be that he, a Jerusalemite with both Israeli and Palestinian friends, could maintain analytic distance? It was only possible, he said, because he was fortunate enough not to have his life disrupted in the way as those he knew who lost loved ones, whose whole lives were thrown. He counted his blessings, and one of them was analytic distance. And this made me want to talk to him all the more.

Bernie is a writer, a professor, a longtime Jerusalem resident. He lives half the year in New Hampshire, where he teaches at Dartmouth College, but his intellectual center is Israel, which he's been writing about for over fifty years. He has spent decades building the case for what he calls the Hebrew Republic: a vision of Israel as a liberal, democratic,

Hebrew-speaking nation that draws on its Jewish heritage without being governed by rabbinic versions of it. A society where individuals regard Torah culture and its commandments as material for personal artistic and ethical struggle, and even policy inspiration, while not being constricted by the decision making culture that evolved in diasporic Judaism. His book of the same name (*The Hebrew Republic*) sits at my bedside for years, among the pile of books I turn to to gain inspiration. He is one of the most thoughtful people I know from the liberal democratic camp, one of a few who have positive visions for Israel and for the region. And he is not a man who suffers fools, which is why he dismisses the argument that the destruction of Gaza – which he acknowledges – is in any way a unique historical phenomenon that must reflect on the Jews for evermore.

"I don't think it makes a lot of sense to talk about what Gaza means for, quote unquote, Jewish power and Jewish fate. I don't think we were ever really a light unto the nations. In modern times, we were simply trying to catch up. And I'm not one of those people who say, well, because of Leviticus 19 (*"love the stranger")*, you know, because we were strangers in the land of Egypt, therefore we should know better. No. I don't think we ever knew better. I don't think humans ever know better. We had a tradition that, in certain ways, lent itself to liberal ideas, yes, especially as we all emerged from medieval ideas. But the notion that we have a special purchase on an ethical life...I've never bought that."

He paused.

"In other words, I don't think that we have a monopoly on some version of ethical life which makes the violence of Gaza peculiarly a crisis for Jews. I think Gaza should be a crisis for any society. And I think the way we've conducted ourselves in Gaza is something that any society that has the kind of military capacities we have would have to grapple with."

I had to admit that until he said those words, I hadn't zoomed out and thought about the destruction of Gaza as a generic thing, not tied to the identities of the parties involved. I was so wrapped up in our particular story, our particular conflict, that I didn't take the time to ask: how would another people, another nation, wrestle with the moral and ethical implications of wide-scale destruction of civilian infrastructure, the killing of thousands of innocents? Even given the way Hamas had embedded itself behind such infrastructure and hid amidst those innocents, what would another nation have done – or felt if it did the same as we did?

Until this conversation with Bernie, I had thought about the destruction of Gaza in the same way many of Israel's critics had: from a uniquely Jewish perspective. What did our choice to destroy Gaza mean about us? What it says about what we learned over the millennia? How does this fit with our perception of power and agency and destiny? These were the questions raised by Beinart and Burg and amplified by the English-speaking media, and I entered the conversation with Bernie hoping to answer them.

So I insisted, for the sake of argument, that perhaps there was something uniquely Jewish about the question of Jewish power and its application, and asked him whether the ethical tradition those who opposed Israel's war in Gaza drew from that was inherent in Judaism, something in the culture itself, or whether such a tradition developed because of circumstance. Because of exile, because of powerlessness, because Jews had no choice but to develop an ethics of the weak.

"I think it's a little of both," he said. But he quickly pushed us to move beyond. Yes, Jewish ethics did have what to say about just and unjust wars. It did place limits of power. But if you look to the tradition, there was always one point put up against the other. "There was contention. There were debates. The idea that we're supposed to argue about things. The idea that there are multiple interpretations and that none of them is final. And that kind of made us maybe a little more comfortable with liberal ideas in the end of the nineteenth century than other people." It did not, however, mean that we were uniformly opposed to the use of power.

Bernie's point, as I have come to understand it (and agree with it), is that it is true that there is a body of ideas that can be called Jewish ethics, a conversation on morality using Jewish traditions and sources. But those ethics – Jewish ethics – are not uniform, nor are they fixed. It makes no sense to disconnect Jewish ethics from the ethics debated among other peoples and traditions because, for at least four centuries, we have been key players in the global conversation about ethics and morality.

Moreover, our own thinking about ethics, about morality, about our identity as Jews, about the human relationship with the Creator and Creation, have all been developed in response and reaction to the world we experienced as Jews. In relation with the other nations and traditions that were not always kind to us.

And that is exactly what is happening now. The idea that Gaza represents the end of Jewish ethics struck him as absurd – "fatuous" was the word he used. Jewish ethics is always evolving in dialogue with our surroundings, with the nations of the world. Every generation works it out anew. The tradition of contention is at the core of our experience as a people, perhaps one of our unique characteristics. As is the epistemology of doubt. Argumentation is at the heart of our relationship with the Eternal and with each other, reflecting our recognition that morality is not absolute, but relative and to be debated. And the very fact that Israelis are agonizing over what was done in their name is itself a product of that tradition. This is what the tradition does. It forces you to grapple. It does not give you clean answers.

This is why Bernie refuses to grant Jews special standing in either direction. Not uniquely virtuous. Not uniquely fallen. A people like other peoples, with a tradition that forces them to grapple with what they've done – what we've done – and a state that, like other states, is capable of terrible things in war.

"Gaza is our Dresden," he said. "[World War II] was a just war. But the firebombing of Dresden was a war crime. The firebombing of Tokyo was a war crime. Hiroshima and the atom bomb, that's a more difficult question. But what I mean is: the fact that the war was just doesn't mean that everything done in the prosecution of the war was just. Those are two different questions. And we have to be able to hold them both."

It struck me, listening to him, that the comparison carried within it something Bernie did not spell out but clearly intended: the Allies are not defined by Dresden. Today's Germany does not define its identity by what was done to Germans at Dresden. The world is better for the defeat of Nazi Germany, even though the way it was achieved included terrible actions and terrible civilian losses. That is the tragic nature of war. Things could have been done differently. Maybe. Probably. But this is what nations do in wars, which is why wars should be avoided, and why the aggressor, the side that starts the war, bears responsibility for what the war does to its own population.

"I think that there are ways in which we were not careful enough in the first few months. But I completely understand the importance of establishing a foothold in Gaza and doing what needed to be done to do that, in a way that would minimize casualties to our own soldiers. And I take it for granted (and here's where I feel callous), I take it for granted that there are going to be a great number of civilian casualties. And I don't believe that that can really be pinned on the Israeli army. That is just what Hamas wanted."

He described the infrastructure Hamas had built, which we have all seen pictures of since: the tunnels under hospitals, the weapons stored in schools, the command centers embedded in residential neighborhoods. War fought in those conditions will produce horrific civilian casualties. There is no version of urban warfare against an enemy that has woven itself into the civilian population that does not. He acknowledged that different approaches could have been used: more precision, more intelligence-led operations, more time. But each alternative carried its own trade-offs. More time meant more risk to soldiers, more precision meant slower progress and a longer war, and a longer war meant more suffering in different ways. There was no clean approach. There were only trade-offs.

Then Bernie made a point that I had not heard anyone else make so directly: the rest of the region wanted Israel to win. The Saudis, the Emiratis, the Egyptians, the Jordanians. The entire Sunni world, he said, was quietly rooting for Israel to finish the job. Nobody in the region wanted Hamas to survive this. They all invest heavily in their own battles against the Muslim Brotherhood, based on their own experiences suffering at their hands.

"But by May of 2024, certainly by June of 2024 when Rafah was taken, and absolutely by the fall of 2024 after Hezbollah was neutered and a few weeks later Assad fell, there was absolutely no excuse to continue the war. None. Zero. By that point, the surgery was done. What we needed was immunotherapy. And instead of immunotherapy, the government kept cutting."

His voice sharpened.

"I believe that the government engaged in a strategy that presumed nothing more than deterrence, preemption, and intimidation. And they had no other arrow in their quiver. Nothing for the region. Nothing for us as a people. Nothing for the Palestinians, who are neighbors and are not going away. Nothing but the idea of intimidation, preemption, and deterrence."

The want of diplomatic imagination, he said, was so profound it amounted to a kind of strategic nihilism. A nihilism embodied by Prime Minister Benjamin Netanyahu.

"When Netanyahu says only the strong survive, he's basically beginning with the classical first premise of fascism. Only the strong survive. That's why you need capitalism, to be rich, because you need riches to buy arms and technology to make the arms more refined. It's a classically fascist idea."

This, Bernie insisted, is not a peculiarly Jewish assumption. It is not rooted in Jewish tradition or Jewish thought. It is a generic strongman ideology that could belong to any nationalist movement anywhere in the world: the idea that the world is a jungle, that strength is the only currency that matters, that diplomacy is weakness. The fact that Israel has succumbed to this ideology under Netanyahu says nothing special about Jews and everything about what happens to any society that lives under siege long enough.

"He's a wonderful cartoonist, Netanyahu. He's somebody whose lines are never wrong. It's just everything he leaves out is what makes it such a cartoon. He leaves out half the world. And when he writes a caption, it's just right. You know, 'They want to destroy us.' That's a great caption. But the cartoon, when you stand back and look at it, doesn't include any of the complexities we've been talking about."

Listening to Bernie, I found myself thinking about something I had tried to communicate to Israel's critics throughout the war: the more the world battered Israel over Gaza, the more it was condemned and isolated and dragged before international courts, the more Israelis grew committed to the war. Bernie helped me understand the mechanism that made it so: the incessant and single-minded condemnation poured on Israel by the international community fed the very siege mentality that Netanyahu exploited, helping him convince Israelis that we were up against the world. Yet every UN resolution, every ICC warrant, every campus protest, colluded with Netanyahu, confirming the cartoon that the world wants to destroy Israel. And the more Israelis felt isolated, the more they coalesced around the street wisdom stating that only the strong survive.

Bernie's point is that if we want to avoid such spiraling in the future, if we really want Israel to recognize that violence is not the answer, if we want Israelis to vote in a government that does not immediately turn to a military solution to every conflict, then the answer is not indiscriminate international pressure. It is normalization. And while the international community may not see this, Israel's neighbors already do.

"This is the first time in the history of Israel that the entire region has said, in advance: we will recognize you. We will normalize relations with you. And you will have normal relations not just with us, but with the entire Islamic world, all the way to Indonesia. All you have to do is show good faith toward some pathway to Palestinian independence."

That Netanyahu was throwing this opportunity away made Bernie incredulous.

"The Saudis are saying it. The Emirates are saying it. Even the Qataris, after a fashion. The Jordanians are desperate for it. The Egyptians need it," Bernie argued. But that is not enough, I pushed back, because Israelis do not compare themselves to their neighbors. Don't seek their approval. Israelis compare themselves to Europeans, Americans. To the elites of the Global North, not the Oil Kingdoms of the Global South. For Israel to feel there is a real path to normalization, I argued, it would need to hear from the elites they look up to that they are committed to Israel's right to exist and will back it in deeds, not only words, by taking on those parties who continue to seek its elimination.

That may be the case, Bernie acknowledged, but it does not excuse how we've responded to the clearly articulated offers of normalization from the leadership of our region. It does not explain the Netanyahu government's public dismissal of those entreaties. "Our only answer to them, again, is intimidation. I find it nothing short of pathetic. Pathetic is the word. Not evil; pathetic. A failure of imagination so complete that it becomes a kind of moral failure."

Normalization, he argues, is the only way to break the siege psychology that is strangling the country. If Israelis could fly to Riyadh just as readily as they fly to Athens, if there were Saudi investment in Israeli tech just as there is Chinese, if there were joint water projects with Jordan that the people of Jordan celebrated as their own, if Palestinians joined the Emiraties in recognizing the existence of Israel alongside them as neighbors with a shared destiny, Israelis could begin to feel that they don't have to live in a permanent state of siege. The trauma of being repeatedly attacked in existential wars could begin to heal. That is the prize. That is what is on the table. And it is being thrown away for the settlements and for Netanyahu's political survival.

Bernie believes Netanyahu and his people knew this scenario was indeed possible, and worked against it.

"By the fall of 2024, Hamas was on its back foot, and we should have begun putting international forces in there, with Palestinian Authority (PA)'s blessing, so that everyone would know we were moving toward some kind of Palestinian independence. Not a full state tomorrow. A pathway. A direction."

And everyone who mattered was saying it.

"Bogie Ya'alon was saying it," he said, mentioning the former Israeli general who was prominent in the Likud for years. "Golan was saying it," mentioning the former Israeli general now leading Israel's leftwing Democrats party. "Gallant was hinting at it," he said, citing the former Israeli general who served as Netanyahu's minister of defense during and after October 7th, until he was fired by Netanyahu for not permitting continued ultra-Orthodox draft evasion. "The entire INSS – Institute for National Security Studies, the hawks, like Amos Yadlin – were saying it. Everybody I talked to and wrote about was saying: go for the deal. The security establishment was practically begging the government to take yes for an answer."

But they didn't. Because taking yes would mean giving up the card Netanyahu has used for years, a card the international community readily gave him every time Israel was unfairly targeted in the media, every time the UN held a special session about Israel and not Sudan or Iran or the Congo, every time a European leader singled out Israel while signing a deal with China.

I asked Bernie whether he thought it was inevitable for someone like Netanyahu to manipulate Israeli public opinion given the circumstances, whether populists like Netanyahu would always win in a society under siege, whether the strongman would always beat the liberal.

"No," he said. "It's not inevitable. But liberals always have a hard sell."

He answered with a line I will never forget.

"Every seven-year-old is an adorable little fascist."

I laughed out loud.

"It's true. The world is what I want it to be. My daddy is the strongest. My mommy is the most beautiful. My family is the best. Our neighborhood is the best. Our team is the best. These are all fascist ideas, right? The idea that the world should be organized around me and my tribe. And graduating from that to a willingness to live with the disturbances of adult mystery, adult uncertainty, freedom – which requires a willingness to fail, to be hurt, to be rejected, to have people say no to you and get up and try again – all of these things are hard. Liberals always have a hard sell."

He explained why populists and especially the populist right has a structural advantage in any society under siege.

"The worst problem we have is the call for solidarity. A country under siege is often going to have demagogues who call for solidarity. And they're always, in effect, calling for solidarity around those points of most broad-based agreement, like Pesach, like halacha, like the idea that we're all one family. The right is able to say: what brings us together is the book. That's what has always kept the Jews together, right? And like, you celebrate Pesach, don't you? You fast on Yom Kippur, right? So what's the big deal? Come home. Put on tefillin. Be with us."

He smiled grimly.

"It takes a certain amount of sophistication and persistence to throw Spinoza at somebody who's telling you to put on tefillin. Somebody says put on tefillin, it takes ten seconds. Explain Spinoza to the person who's telling you to put on tefillin? That takes a couple of hours. And at the end of the two hours, they look at you and say: so are you going to put on tefillin or not?"

He laughed. But he was not joking. And he is not wrong. Because it isn't about putting on tefillin – the traditional arm wrapping religious Jews don each morning for their early prayers. And it isn't to dismiss solidarity; solidarity itself is a good thing, when it is based on mutuality and not conformity. What I understood him to mean is that the challenge we face is rooted in the liberal tendency to cede the ground on values – itself a new thing, since liberals didn't get to the top of the food chain by being nice. Yet something went awry along the way, and now it seems that liberals do not know when to argue for what they believe in, when to reject the framing presented by populists who weave a narrative based on the threads of tradition to entrap our minds and curtail our political horizon.

I feel I should explain this further, because I've come to understand this as a central idea expressed best by Bernie but coming through most of the conversations that led to this book: Israel's liberal democratic forces are facing the same struggles as many other liberal democracies. The difference is that we are doing so at the same time as we are beset by external threats to our existence. This makes it all the more difficult for Israelis to win in either struggle.

There's something else: As Shany Mor, a writer and public intellectual, pointed out to me, our post-modern liberal societies have a tendency to bend the knee to ideas they label 'authentic,' when they are, in fact, contemporary expressions of traditions and customs used to further a political position that often undermine the values that make our societies free. To use Bernie's example, the young men who offer to wrap men in tefillin across Israeli public squares are funded by political parties who market their version of orthodox Judaism as the only legitimate Judaism, and then use that claim to justify political demands such as full subsidies for yeshiva students and a pass from serving in the Army. Too many Israelis have no other exposure to Jewish religious practice, and have come to believe that the Judaism these young men represent is, indeed, authentic. The ultra-Orthodox parties in Israel use that foot in secular Israel's mental door to advance their political agenda and corrupt Israel's political system.

Yet the current form of Israel's ultra-Orthodox Judaism is a product of Israel's political system, radically different than it was even the span of my lifetime. As Rabbi Yosef Kaminer, an ultra-Orthodox member of the Gur sect explained to me, it wasn't until the 1980s that ultra-Orthodox society evolved into what we see today in Israel: the idea of the "Society of Learners," a social system built around public subsidies where men learned and women worked, and where no-one served the State that paid their bills. This reality was only made possible by the political deal made by the government Menahem Begin formed in 1977. Until then, the ultra-Orthodox were just another ingredient in the Israeli melting pot, none more authentic than the rest. By making a deal with the ultra-

Orthodox, Begin, as had Israel's first prime minister David Ben Gurion before him, Israel's liberal society willingly contracted its self-definition to the secular realm, and left spiritual authenticity to be defined by the rabbinic monopoly. Today's struggles to get the ultra-Orthodox to serve, to work – and their struggle to achieve greater gender separation in Israel, further curtailment of individual freedoms on marriage and divorce – are the result of that deal made less than half a century ago.

Same can be said, to give a Western example, for how elites across the Global North tip toe around radical Islam. The best example I can give of this is that nearly every single marketing material put out by non-governmental organizations or governments seeking to present diversity will include at least one picture of a woman wearing a hijab, the traditional hair covering of religious Islam. To be clear: women should have the right to wear a hijab, just as men should have the right to wear a kippah – both are marks of religiosity that I believe human beings have the right to bear. Yet it is also important to note that there are many Muslim societies around the world who do not require their women to cover their hair, and one should also note that many Muslim states force their women to cover their hair whether they would like to or not. One can assume that many of those Muslim women feel as the Iranian women do, that forcing them to publicly mark their fealty is a blow against their personhood. By making a hijab-wearing woman a fixture of diversity literature, I fear that liberal societies have taken a side in the battle for equality between men and women, ceding ground to Islamists who would have women recognize their place. By acting as if a hijab is somehow an authentic sign of Middle Eastern identity, instead of having it be as common in NGO pamphlet imagery as men with kippot.

This, of course, has direct implications on the West's relationship with Israel. Because once Western elites are socialized into thinking that the truest expression of Middle Eastern identity is a woman in a hijab – itself a symbol of fundamentalism and a claim to authenticity and authority – then claims made by the leaders of those 'authentic' minorities' that Israel is a foreign entity are given precedence. Just like the young men offering tefillin serve as a gateway to ultra-Orthodox political maneuvering, the young women piously covering their hair has served as the most visible marker for Islamist positions, obscuring the fact that the Middle East has been the home of myriad cultures and traditions conquered and settled and colonized and homogenized by the Arab armies of Islam.

In my opinion, the liberal position, the leftist position should be to strengthen those same minorities who have managed to survive the conquest, to free them from the very oppression we see on display when women are forced to cover their hair. To make the case for freedom, and to reject claims of the authority of authenticity. To struggle for the right of a people to remake themselves, to evolve, into the nation they want to be, informed by the past but not enslaved by it.

One of those peoples who have survived millennia of conquest and oppression and forced conversion and assimilation campaigns and evolved in its traditions and customs and approaches to the world are the Jews. Or, as Bernie puts it, the Hebrews. And I believe that the liberal answer to the illiberal push to homogenize the region is to support the development of what Bernie calls the Hebrew Republic.

The Hebrew Republic Bernie envisions is a state for the Hebrew people. A state like all the other states, a nation like all the other nations, which is to say unique and distinct and special like each and every nation feels it is as well. A state with a political system which makes mistakes, sometimes horrible ones, with a nation that has as much a right to correct those mistakes as any other.

"This Hebrew nation is going to have some people who are reactionary and some people who are democrats, and this Hebrew nation is going to have a culture war of its own." Beneath it all, this Hebrew Republic should be recognized not by its politics, not by its leaders, but by its art. Its culture. Its values, drawn from an ancient well whose waters continue to flow through the present day.

"The Hebrew language was nobody's mother tongue a hundred and fifty years ago. Nobody spoke it at home. It was a liturgical language, a language of prayer and study. And now it's a language in which people argue about parking tickets and write love poems and curse at each other in traffic. It's such an achievement, to create a Hebrew-speaking civil society where individuals with liberal imagination can go back into the masoret, into the tradition, and pull out stuff that they can use in a poem or a pop song or a Supreme Court decision."

He named names every Israeli knows: Yehuda Amichai. Leah Goldberg. And then he told me about Matti Caspi, whose work I knew less well.

"Matti Caspi has this song, '*Makom le Daagah*,' *A Place of Worry*. He takes the God of the liturgy, from prayer, and puts him in a pop song. A being cursed with being all knowing, seeing the human future, sitting in a far corner of the 'Garden,' and fretting. He turns God into a character. Not the God of the Rabbinate. A personal God. An intimate God. A God you can empathize with on the radio."

He leaned forward.

"The profoundly political implications of that. Taking the *masoret*, the tradition, and reversing it. Secularizing it. Making it art. Making it yours. That's what this Hebrew-speaking civil society does. That's what a pop song can do in a language that was liturgical a hundred and fifty years ago."

"If Peter Beinart doesn't understand the profoundly political implications of a song like this, if he's never heard of the singer Yehudit Ravitz or the poet Leah Goldberg or the comic Lior Schleien, he doesn't understand the grandeur of it. The beauty of it. The reality of it and the complexity of it. He's looking at Israel from the outside and seeing a conflict and a version of Jewish narrowed by American experience. I'm looking at it from the inside and seeing a civilization."

A civilization that has as much to give humanity as any other.

"Israeli life can assimilate people to a culture that is distinctly Jewish – historically distinctly Jewish – the way America is English. But not English in the sense of high church. Not English in the sense of the Mayflower. English in the sense that the language carries the culture, and the culture is open to anyone who enters it. A Hebrew-speaking society that can be inclusive of Arabs, of Ukrainian Christians, of the children of Filipino workers. They may come up with a literature in Hebrew that adds to our life. Like Philip Roth and Saul Bellow added to the world of Anglo life."

I thought, listening to him, about the children of migrant workers I have met in Tel Aviv, kids born to Filipino or Eritrean or Thai parents who speak perfect Hebrew, who went to Israeli schools, who did national service. The ones I would see riding their bikes on Yom Kippur, laughing and insulting each other in the most up-to-date Hebrew slang. They are as Israeli as anyone I know. They argue in Hebrew, they joke in Hebrew, they dream in Hebrew. They are living proof that the Hebrew Republic is not a theory. It is already happening, in the schools and streets of south Tel Aviv, in the army units where Ethiopian-Israeli and Russian-Israeli and Druze soldiers serve together. The question is whether the state will recognize what the culture has already produced.

Bernie pointed to the Arab citizens of Israel who write in Hebrew, to Sayed Kashua, to Anton Shammas, as evidence that a Hebrew-speaking civil society can absorb and be enriched by people who are not ethnically Jewish. "The Supreme Court has gone back and forth about this, but still seems unable to define Jew in national terms, so that all can be included, and be thought equal, as any democratic society requires. Israel seems the only country on earth that won't recognize itself – in part to pander to the Israeli rabbinate – and to American Jews who need a vicarious identity.

"We have a nation here," he said. "And that's such a goddamn achievement. That's what we have to protect. That's what we have to fight for. Not the settlements. Not the rabbinate. Not Greater Israel. This. The language. The culture. The possibility."

He paused.

"We cannot be a little Jewish Pakistan here. That's what's at stake. And the fight for Israeliness, for the Hebrew Republic, for the idea that this is a nation defined by its language and its culture and its democratic institutions, not by its rabbinate, is also the fight for democracy. They're the same fight."

Just as the fight for Jewish self-determination and Palestinian self-determination are the same fight. "It's like a Pew survey asking Americans: are you more sympathetic to Israelis or more sympathetic to Palestinians? As if there are no Israelis who are sympathetic to Palestinians. As if there are no

Palestinian citizens of Israel. It reduces the whole thing to a cartoon – there's that word again – two sides, pick one."

What stays with me from my conversation with Bernie is the insistence on normalcy. Humanity. He refused to treat the destruction of Gaza as a uniquely Jewish catastrophe, as the end of Jewish civilization or the proof that Zionism was a failed movement and Israel has no moral right to exist. It was a brutal war, a terrible one, a war fought the way wars are often fought, led by a self-obsessed political class willing to do horrible things to retain power despite the terrible consequences it produced.

By broadening his lens and recognizing this pattern in history he refused to treat Israel as a uniquely fallen state. As a destroyed civilization. It was, and perhaps when you're reading these lines it still is, a country under siege, captured by a strongman ideology that any society under siege might produce. Most importantly, he refused to treat the way out as uniquely impossible. The regional deal is on the table, the liberal tradition is a real alternative backed by the majority of Israelis, the Hebrew nation exists and is an achievement worth fighting for.

I found it helpful to think of Gaza as our Dresden. A war crime executed during a just war. Just as the Allies were not defined by Dresden, we need not be defined by Gaza. We should be defined instead by what comes after – how we build a better future for Israelis, for Palestinians, for all of the humans in our region impacted by our actions and influenced by our power.

To do so, however, I fear we will first need to win the struggle for liberalism. Because without winning internally, we may become the little Jewish Pakistan Bernie described. Or a Jewish Republic in the mold of Iran's Islamic Republic. The fight for the Hebrew Republic – for a nation defined by language and culture and democratic institutions rather than by theocracy and settlements – is the fight for democracy itself. It will require those of us who believe in the potential of Israel as a nation as unique as all the others, with the potential to contribute like all the others, to fight for those values and not cede the stage to the populist forces of fundamentalism and authoritarianism.

That fight will take generations. Bernie has been fighting it for fifty years. He is not going anywhere. Neither should we.

Naama Klar

"Nobody is coming. I need to save my children myself."

Naama Klar arrived at this understanding on the morning of October 7th. It stayed with her throughout the war.

"From that moment, 'nobody is coming' keeps repeating in my head. Because I suddenly understand that, in the big sense of the crisis, what we won't do, nobody will do for us. There is no responsible adult."

Naama lives in Jaffa, on the southern edge of Tel Aviv. She works in the field of Jewish Peoplehood: the professional field devoted to strengthening Jewish identity, community, and connection across the Diaspora. She runs educational programs for ANU, what was once known as the Diaspora Museum at Tel Aviv University, one of my favorite places in the world. She is completing a doctorate at Gratz College in Philadelphia. She is raising young children in a city that, as she puts it, does not adapt itself to her needs.

She is also, by her own reckoning, the optimal citizen. It's hard to argue with her assessment.

"I don't cost the state money. I'm a healthy person. I take care of my children. I don't cause accidents. I pay all my insurance on time. I am the optimal citizen. If you were to sketch the dream citizen, it's me. It's my family."

And yet.

"Despite being the number one citizen, nobody pays attention to me. Nobody bothers to adapt to my needs. I'm a mother of young children. Tel Aviv is one of the most expensive and most difficult cities in Israel. The city doesn't adapt to me. They don't give me the basic conditions to grow my family without stress and anxiety. I can't even walk on a sidewalk [because of parked cars]. It's just a daily thing, but still."

She told me this without self-pity. It was an observation, delivered with the analytical tone of someone who has spent thousands of hours thinking about systems, strategies, tactics, and the responsibilities of public service.

"No one represents us. There's no one to vote for. I thought about running myself in Tel Aviv on issues of young mothers and families. I can't: I have kids. How am I going to sit in meetings from noon and do this for free? So there's no voice, no party or politician that represents where I find myself. In the political space, who I am and what I bring to the table doesn't matter. This is in contrast to every other space in my life."

I understand just how infuriating that is for Naama, who is someone who has devoted her life to Israel, to the Jewish People. I first met Naama nearly two decades ago in Jerusalem, where she joined the Steering Committee for the PresenTense Fellowship there. As a young activist she was devoted to the city, to making it livable for the plurality that calls the city home. I followed her career as she worked through the ranks at the Reut Institute, a policy think tank founded by Gidi Grinstein that brought together so many of Israel's finest recent University graduates to develop new approaches to Israel's policy challenges and connect Israel to the Jewish world at large. More recently I got to know her again through her role at ANU. There, Naama heads the Koret School for Jewish Peoplehood. And there, two days before October 7th, on October 5th, something happened that shook me when she shared it.

The Codex Sassoon, the oldest complete Torah manuscript in the world, had arrived in Israel. It had been donated to the National Library for thirty-eight million dollars. But before it would go there, Naama and her team decided they would give it the greeting it deserved.

"That Friday, my whole team went to the reception at Ben Gurion airport. We received the most expensive Jewish book I've ever heard of. I felt very strong. I felt very strong as a Jewish woman, as an Israeli."

And she remembers that on that same day, one of ANU's senior educators was leading a group through the building. A grandmother had brought her grandchildren to learn about the Holocaust. The children were young. After walking through the Holocaust exhibition on the second floor, they were shaken. The educator knelt down and told them:

"Children, this is truly very scary. It was a very hard time. But you don't need to worry. Now we're here, in the State of Israel. Nothing like this will happen."

"Two days later, October 7th. The educator went looking for the grandmother and the children to apologize. Because she had told them that, and then it happened."

She shook her head.

"But it's not her fault. It's the Zionist narrative that shaped her and was embedded in everything: the textbooks, the Independence Day ceremonies, the entire story. The narrative that here there would be no Holocaust. That Jewish history ended with the establishment of the state and is no longer cyclical. That narrative broke."

The night before the attack, Naama and her family had been thinking about the provocations expected around Simchat Torah. This was due to hostilities that broke out only days before, during Yom Kippur prayers in Tel Aviv, between a religious outreach group that set up gender segregated prayers in one of the city's main public squares and secular activists fighting against religious coercion. That was the type and scale of threat she was calibrating for: an internal rift among the Jews, another crack in Jewish Peoplehood. She was certain that the only thing that could destroy Israel was if Israelis destroyed it from within. The idea of an external breach, of the border falling, of the state simply not showing up, was not in her calculations.

And then came the morning.

"First thing: a survivalist effect. I immediately understood: nobody is coming. I need to save my children myself."

Her husband was called up to the reserves. She was alone with the children in Jaffa.

"I'm ready," she told me she remembers thinking. "Weapon, ability to lock ourselves in, food, water, everything I need to survive."

She began calculating. Three days on her own. What food they had. Where the shelter was. What she would do if the situation in Jaffa itself deteriorated – a mixed city, Jewish and Arab, where she had lived through previous rounds of violence.

"In Jaffa, during previous wars, the Arabs would set off fireworks and clap. You could hear it. You knew what it meant. It was in celebration."

She paused.

"Not on October 7th. They were with us."

This surprised her. Not because she thought her Arab neighbors were enemies before that day. She lives in Jaffa alongside Arab citizens of Israel for years, worked alongside Arab Israelis, and taught Arab Israelis and learned from Arab Israelis. But despite all that she feared the pattern of previous conflicts would reemerge: the fireworks, the clapping, the ambient threat that comes when your neighbors celebrate what terrifies you.

"On October 7th, that didn't happen. The Arab Israelis passed the test. They chose Israel's side, broadly. They want their future with Israel. That was real. That was significant."

I asked Naama what else changed for her after October 7th. She told me three things.

"I'll organize it like this. There are three things that completely changed. Who I was before October 7th is no longer relevant. I swapped three mindsets. First, nobody is coming. There is no IDF. They weren't there. There is no IDF. There's me. I'll protect my children." Yet the 'nobody' she was referring to meant the government, not the people: Naama remains impressed and heartened by the people, those who make up the nation of Israel, who took responsibility for their lives in response to the attacks, and took action to care for the wellbeing of their neighbors in the shadow of the more terrible days in our history.

The second change for her was her recognition of the price of being Jewish.

"The crisis of October 7th is not a crisis of the Gaza envelope [the towns and villages and kibbutzim living in the region proximate to Gaza]. It's a global Jewish crisis. Being Jewish was an awesome thing for many years. But from October 7th, for the foreseeable future (which I estimate at a decade, decade and a half) it's going to be very hard to be Jewish. Sad, amazing, but with a price tag. And dangerous."

The third was the loyalty test.

"Not all the Jews who entered the crisis with us were with us at the end of the crisis. October 7th is a loyalty test for the Jewish People. Everyone is being tested. Everyone." And with this Naama counts the Jews who distanced themselves from Israel after October 7th abroad, the ultra-Orthodox who protest against service despite seeing why Israel needs the able bodied to serve.

These three realizations are nearly paralyzing when taken together, and a good summary of what so many have felt: Nobody is coming. It's dangerous to be Jewish. Your own people may abandon you. Naama could have retreated into despair or rage, as many did. Instead, she did what she always does: she diagnosed the problem and started working on how to fix it.

Because alongside the three things that broke, Naama saw things that held.

The Arab Israelis in Jaffa held, as they did across the country. The fireworks she and many others had braced for never came. Instead, her neighbors were quiet, present, choosing a shared future. Many volunteered to help the wounded, to provide care, to support efforts to fill the vacuum left by the government's absence. Israel literally could not have recovered without them. She saw this not as a one-off but as part of a larger pattern: the Abraham Accords, the growing integration of Arab citizens into Israeli professional life, the realization among Arab Israelis that their future was bound to the state's.

"That's a real asset," she told me. "It's not sentimental. It's strategic. Arab Israeli society made a choice. We should take that seriously and build on it."

And civil society held. While the state collapsed on the morning of October 7th, while the IDF was absent, while the government was paralyzed, while the political leadership that had spent a year tearing the country apart over judicial reform was nowhere to be found, ordinary Israelis organized themselves. When nobody official came, we came for each other.

"Within hours, there were civilian command centers. People collecting food, driving south, housing evacuees. WhatsApp groups that turned into logistics networks overnight. Nobody told them to do this. Nobody authorized it. They just did it. Because nobody was coming, so they became the ones who came."

And that provided her with evidence that something, beneath it all, was all right.

"Civil society in Israel is incredibly strong. Incredibly strong. The state failed, and the people didn't. That tells you something. The capacity is here. The leadership isn't in the Knesset. It's in the communities, the NGOs, the professional networks, the reservists who organized themselves in parking lots."

And yet, that isn’t how it is supposed to be. Democracies function only when the leadership reflects both the will of the people and aligns with the needs of the people. That leadership arises spontaneously at the grassroots should be celebrated. But without leadership on the political level, the most we can hope for are local fixes as opposed to strategic direction.

This question of leadership has consumed her, and she came to believe the failure was a systems problem, not a personnel problem.

"The basic principle of political economy: people, systems, even nature, respond to incentives and constraints. The design of the incentives determines the conduct. Systems that reward value-based leadership will have value-based leadership. In systems that reward not taking responsibility, people won't take responsibility."

Systems that decouple leadership from the people can't fix themselves. They need to be fixed by the people. By their demands. "What we need is for the people who organized the civilian response on October 7th – the ones who built the command centers, who drove south, who housed the evacuees – to understand that they are the leaders. They already proved it. Now they need to step into that role permanently."

She has been taking that lesson with her everywhere.

"I sit in meetings now with deputy ministers and I say: look right, look left, look up. There is nobody. There's you and me. Whatever we decide to do, that's what will happen. No other person is coming to do this work. That's terrifying. It's also liberating. Because it means the people in the room can actually make something happen."

But then there are decisions only the political class can make, ones that affect all of us, that have led to a reaction by the world that has put increasing pressure on the Jewish People, and have made it harder to be a Jew. So I asked Naama about the destruction of Gaza. The scale of it, how she processed it morally. How it affects her thinking about our responsibility as a people to each other, to our future.

"Really easy," she said. "I give all the responsibility to Hamas. Maybe that's not fair, but analytically it works. If you booby-trap a building, it will be taken down. That's your problem. If you put a baby as a human shield, that's also your fault. Whoever doesn't accept international norms upon themselves is not entitled to benefit from them. I say this as a moral statement."

She paused.

"But within that framework, things that weren't okay? The threats of starvation? That was wrong. That was forbidden. And the genocidal statements our elected officials make? They should be in jail. Someone who says let's drop an atomic bomb on Gaza and doesn't understand where Gaza is or what an atomic bomb is or what he's supposed to be saying? That's treason."

Her husband was finishing his fifth round of reserve duty. He texted her from inside Gaza.

"He tells me stories from Gaza now. When you're in Gaza, you forget what's normal. It's a lot. It's a lot to read those texts. They're insane things, truly. Of course he keeps going back to serve. I'm proud. But the stories? They stay with you."

I've heard this sentiment repeated quite a few times in conversations about Gaza, recognizing the tragedy yet placing the responsibility on the aggressor.

I have to say, I only partially buy it.

I recently read Orson Scott Card's *Ender's Game* to my daughter. For those who haven't yet read it, read it. As a partial spoiler, the book follows the path of Ender, a boy genius recruited by the forces of humanity to take on an alien threat. Throughout his training Ender ends up in crisis after crisis, bullied by boys who are jealous of him and his abilities. Time after time Ender is attacked, only to prevail, and just at the moment where it is clear he has already won he strikes his enemy one more time to ensure he wins not only the current battle but all battles after that. My daughter and I spent many hours debating the ethics of war, the justice of defense, questioning the morality of power and its application. Defining victory in moral terms.

Like Naama, I do recognize that there is a certain wisdom required to recognize that certain situations are irreconcilable, that certain worldviews will ultimately clash unless one side caves in and abandons its commitment to supplanting or expelling the other. I also agree that we, as humans, must forgive ourselves for caring more about the lives of our loved ones than the lives of strangers, especially when those strangers are aligned with the group seeking to harm you and yours. Yet I also believe in the importance of restraint, in the justice of expending just a bit more energy and power and wealth to do whatever it takes to protect the innocent even if they are from the other side.

Which is why I asked Naama to describe to me how she defines victory and who is included in the future she is willing to fight and sacrifice for.

She turned around and took down a bottle of wine from the shelf, and showed me what was written on it.

"We were three weeks at home. Do you remember that? Everybody was at home. And the moment we returned to the office, I took an old bottle of wine out of the closet. A good bottle. And I wrote on it: victory conditions."

She listed three.

"The defeat of Hamas. Peace with Saudi Arabia. And the fall of the Ayatollah regime in Iran."

She put the bottle on the shelf in the office, where everyone could see it, and said that after each of these conditions are met, they would do a L'Chaim.

"People come in – colleagues, partners, visitors – and they see the bottle and they add their own conditions. Someone wrote the return of the hostages. Someone else wrote new elections. It keeps growing. But the original three are mine."

She smiled.

"It sounds naive, maybe. But I need it there. I need to walk into the office every morning and see what we're working toward. Not just surviving the day. Not just managing the crisis. Winning. Actually winning. And I believe we can."

I would hope that any liberal democratic person, any person actually committed to humanist values, would agree to all three of these conditions: Hamas must be defeated if both

Israelis and Palestinians are ever to live in peace. Peace with Saudi Arabia is a prerequisite for peace with the broader Muslim world. And the fall of the Ayatollah's murderous, fundamentalist regime in Iran would free the region, and the world, from one of the greatest exporters of extremist violence. But, so far, we've failed to achieve any of the three. What does that mean for us? I asked her.

"The burden of proof is on our generation to show that Zionism is an endless movement. Not a complete story. Not a chapter that ended with the establishment of the state. An ongoing project that demands new muscles in every generation."

Muscles?

"We call it muscles in crisis. The Jewish People went through very hard things and survived. Not only survived! In coping, we developed capabilities and skills. Jews being wanderers, nomads, for example. It's a funny phenomenon, very widespread, but it also gave us a skill set. Languages, adaptability, commerce, networks. Without being wandering Jews, we wouldn't have what we have today. This period will force us to develop some new Jewish skill set. If we do it from a place of connection to all the advantages we received in the past, we'll be stronger. If we manage to pass this down through memory to future generations, they'll be stronger too."

She told me she had restructured her entire professional life around this one challenge of helping us develop the muscles from our past failures to take on the challenges still before us.

"Everything I do from October 7th until today, professionally, is to ask: in what way can the story of the Jewish People give us value, advantage, or resilience right now? Only that. Anything that doesn't directly answer that brief, I've cut from my portfolio. We're in for a hard decade. The question is whether we develop the muscles or we don't. Whether we build the new story or we let the old broken one keep telling itself. That's the only question."

When I processed my conversation with Naama I kept coming back to the three things that broke for her and the three things that held. The breaking of her belief that someone was coming, that being Jewish was easy, that Jews would stand together and rise together – any one of those breaks could have been fatal to her sense of purpose. To her belief in Jewish Peoplehood.

Instead, she looked at what held. The Arab neighbors who didn't set off fireworks. The civilians who built command centers in parking lots. The reservists who drove south without orders. The professional networks that reorganized overnight. Her husband, returning for a fifth round of duty because somebody had to.

I'd like to think that in retrospect, it was inaccurate to conclude that nobody is coming. Because countless citizens came to the rescue. Not our government, not the army. But optimal citizens like Naama, the ones the state takes for granted, the ones who can't walk on a sidewalk in their own city because of the terrible parking problems and broken streets, the one nobody represents. Turns out they are the ones willing to do the work the state won't do.

These citizens – Jews, Arabs, Israelis all of them, even those migrant workers who came to help with the food logistics centers, helped ferry people to safety – are the embodiment of the Zionist movement, not the State. The Jews abroad who rallied and fundraised and sent equipment and joined missions to lend their hands to the rebuilding, who fought to protect Jews on campuses, who donated to ensure Israel had the resources to protect its citizens, they too are the Jews who will have a hard decade ahead but are made of the mettle that will survive it. They are the culmination of thousands of years of evolution of a culture born in power, made thoughtful by exile, and reconstructed by the ingathering in the land of their ancestors. The State is but an instrument upon which they play. Those who currently control the state, who were elected to positions of power and worked incessantly to gain more power and ensure their control, do not represent Israel. Only the people who keep showing up for their neighbors, who are willing to put their personal interest aside for the greater good, do.

Yau Levy

Yau Levy found out about the horrific attacks on October 7th from an employee in Kenya.

He was in a cabin in the north of Israel with his wife and their daughter Nova. It was Nova's birthday. They had slept late. His phone buzzed with a message from his Kenyan colleague: Are you okay? Is everything all right? If she was asking, something very bad must have happened, Yau figured.

He started reading the news. He saw immediately that it was something enormous. And he did something that I found, when he described it, almost unbearably intimate.

"I sort of held on for a few minutes, a few seconds, to what had been until now. Because I knew that everything was shattering. I sat alone. I didn't tell my wife yet. My first reaction was a kind of mourning. Mourning for the beauty of Israel. For my private life, for our society up to that moment. And the knowledge that it was all shattering in our faces."

Yau grew up in Israel, born to immigrant parents, his mother from South America, his father from South Africa. Both came as young people through the youth movements, with the intention of making Israel better and stronger. His father had lived through the apartheid regime in Cape Town. His parents are no longer together. His father became religious and moved to a settlement, a fact that Yau mentioned and then paused on, as if aware of the box it might put his father in.

"I very much love and admire my father. And one of the things I admire most about him is his ability to contain complexity. He talks about South Africa. On one hand he was involved in protests against the regime. On the other hand, he also describes the violence that Black people committed, without justifying it but without erasing it either. He even spent time in jail for a crime someone else committed. And today, even though he's a settler, in quotation marks, he has a very complex opinion. Not necessarily one-sided."

He paused.

"I learn enormously from him about this thing, that identity is complex, and history is complex, and it's not black and white. And in the context of how we tell the story, I think the great strength, the greatest success, is if we can tell a story with this complexity."

That word – complexity – came up again and again in our conversation. It is the word that most of the people in this book reach for when they try to describe the thing they feel is missing from the conversation about Israel. As I've come to understand it, when they say holding complexity what they mean is having the ability to reflect upon a world without minimizing or simplifying the players and their many motivations, giving space for each's uniqueness. It is a sign of maturity, of seeing each other's humanity. On the other hand, in the general media, I have heard it used as a means of explaining away the unexplainable. Of seeking to justify the unjustifiable.

Yau used it in a different way: he described complexity not as an adjective, as a way to paper over roughness, not as a way to excuse something, but as a goal. Something to aspire to. Something that should be encouraged. Something that requires specific conditions to flourish, and should be nurtured, because to be complex is better than to imagine the world is simple. His father was his example: a man who could live in a "settlement" and hold anti-apartheid convictions, who could describe violence on all sides without collapsing into a single narrative because he had the confidence to hold contradictions.

Yau's wife is not Jewish. She is English, and she knew nothing about Israel before she met him. Her family and childhood friends are all in England. They met in India, while Yau was on a work trip for my company, MobileODT, where he led the company's AI product to detect cervical cancer, and they spent two days together. Little over half a year later, Yau moved to England to study towards his masters degree in engineering for sustainable development, and they reunited. They haven't separated since.

After his degree, Yau went on to found an incredible company, Rural Senses, which enables international development agencies and governmental and non-governmental organizations to better understand the needs of the people they're seeking to serve. He set up offices across the

African continent, built an organization that does well while doing good. An organization Israel can and should be proud of.

He and his now-wife moved to Israel, were married in a ceremony held in the country, and it was here, in the months after October 7th, that his wife experienced something that Yau, as an Israeli, had spent a lifetime getting used to: friends who came to Israel for their wedding telling her they would never come back; enormous amounts of hate on social media directed towards her and her new home from people she knew. She posted things about what was happening to her, personal updates about how it was to be a human being living in a land torn by war, and received vitriol from people she had thought of as friends. "She said to me: I only now understand that Israelis are the only people who have to be afraid to say where they're from when they're outside their own country. There's no other country where someone asks you where you're from and you're afraid to give the real answer."

She was seeing the world through Israeli eyes for the first time, without the armor Israelis develop over years of exposure. And it was doubly shocking because she had no history, no ideology, no stake in the argument. She was simply a woman from England who had married an Israeli and was now discovering what that meant in the world.

At the same time, Yau rediscovered what it was like to be an Israeli in Israel and what the country could become if only it allowed its good inclination to overcome the bad.

"The initial response of Israelis [to October 7th] was something amazing. Unprecedented mobilization. In my life I've never seen such a thing. So much rallying and so much self-sacrifice from people. The seeds of it were already there before, in the judicial reform protests, every Saturday night, people sacrificing their comfort to protect democracy, to protect what existed. But after October 7th, it went way beyond protests - extraordinary amounts of people took action, innovated, put their lives and personal gains aside and worked day and night to support those in need, source supplies, and speak up for bringing the hostages back and ending the war." Despite the horrific context, Yau describes the uplifting energy at that time. "It reminded me of what I heard from my mom when she came to Israel in the '70s with a group of young idealist people full of selflessness eager to make Israeli society a model society."

He saw in this something essential about Israel. "The caring here is perhaps what differentiates Israelis from many other countries. How much people care about what happens here. The people of Israel are truly devoted to their existence, their freedom, and their opportunity to thrive. It's not something I've found anywhere else. People genuinely care what happens to each other and to the country, as if the whole country is one big extended family," he reflected, then paused. "Not only that, there are also so many talented and capable people here and when many talented people care so much about a cause they change the reality."

But what followed the mobilization was tragedy. Yau watched, along with all of us, how the war ground on, month after month, bringing things the society could barely cope with. Yau was not a military strategist and did not pretend to be one. But he could feel it, the shift from purpose to drift, from justified response to something unmoored.

"I felt the war was not being conducted well. That perhaps if we had healthier, more grounded leadership from the start, the war would have been conducted better and led to better outcomes. Something in the beginning, in the first ground incursion – the urge for revenge, almost indiscriminate – I felt it was not smart. It was not smart, and it truly contradicted the goals of returning the hostages and defeating Hamas."

He stopped to think before continuing.

"Throughout the war, Israel lost its justification. It was no longer clear what Israel was still fighting for. And if we killed our own hostages, then how many innocent Palestinians did we kill in the same way?"

The thing that bothered him most was not the military failures but the absence of any vision for what came after.

"The deliberate avoidance by the government of talking about the day after, of bringing any kind of vision – that's saying, okay, so we fight here and then what? And then we miss the huge potential that a crisis this great has for bringing repair. Instead we stay in this consciousness of conflict every few years, another war. And what does that mean for a child growing up in a place like this? What does it mean, at the level of consciousness, for a state that says I don't fix things, I just live from crisis to crisis? Our leaders never said what yes. Only what no."

"What yes" – in Hebrew, *mah ken* – is a common Hebrew phrase, and is such a wonderful way to encapsulate everything the current leadership refuses to say. Everything for them is a no: No Palestinian state, no concessions, no political process, no day-after plan. "What yes" they avoid, and yet that is what we desperately needed at that troubled time, still need today. What do we actually want? What are we building towards? What is the positive vision that justifies the sacrifice?

"To say "what yes" requires complexity, facing conflicting interests, forces us to deal with uncomfortable facts. Our own government fears dealing with complexity as it can be less popular. But this fear, lack of courage to set a vision of hope, is what keeps us in this never ending cycle."

For the first time in his life, Yau told me, he had considered not living in Israel. Not because of rockets or sirens, but because of the fear of living in a place without hope.

"My wife and I have an informal agreement that says: as long as we see that there is hope here for a better future, we're here. And the day we lose hope, then we won't be here anymore."

He paused.

"I think what will kill Israel is not wars. It's the loss of hope. And in this war they brought us, I think, very close to the loss of hope."

Paradoxically, just as things were getting the worst, Yau caught glimpses of the best yet to come in the activists returning to the streets, the protests reigniting. He found hope, once again, in the people taking their fate into their own hands.

"People are less afraid to express their voice. More willing to fight for the values that made this place what it is today. That's perhaps our strength as Israelis, that even when there is suppression of freedom of thought and expression, people still aren't afraid to express their opinions. There are many, many people and communities expressing themselves and not afraid to express opinions against the narrative."

"I'm very happy to see the people of the protest entering politics. That's the best thing that happened to us politically. A people that knows how to say what it wants! We just need the strong and attentive leaders who will know how to leverage that into long-term changes."

He also saw a shift in the valence of hope closer to home. Yau has a Palestinian colleague he has worked with daily for about six years. On the evening of October 7th, the colleague sent him a message: “I am so ashamed from the photos I have seen, I stand with you brother. Praying for peace and unity.” In the months that followed, the colleague also experienced enormous pain over what Israel was doing in Gaza, in his village in the West Bank, among his people, in his world. Both realities existed inside the same working relationship. Neither man asked the other to choose.

"Both he and I and all the people on our team know how to contain complexity and understand that things have multiple layers and it's not black and white."

This ability to see complexity in action, reflected in the activism of the streets, on display in the dynamics of his team, gives Yau hope. They keep him in Israel, even as he asks himself whether the country as a whole can grow that capacity for complexity, if our neighbors can overcome their own tendency to simplify, if our leadership can adopt a stance founded upon complexity. He believes the answer to each of these is yes, because of what he experienced working on the African continent.

Yau's work is in the Global South. Over the past decade – in MobileODT, during his studies, in Rural Senses – he spent years in places where people were rebuilding after violence, after displacement, after the collapse of trust. What he saw there gave him a framework he believes can help us in our region solve our particular problems.

"I was in very difficult areas in Uganda where people were truly victimized. The people I spoke to were deeply unhappy with their situation. They felt trapped and miserable. And this often led to two different reactions: on one hand, some use it to justify bad deeds: crime, theft, things like that. On the other hand you have people who desire to flee. I had conversations in Uganda where, at the end of a meeting about something else entirely, people would say to me: You live in England, right?

Do you maybe need a housekeeper? A gardener? Take me with you."

Yau learned from that a truth he then applied to the Israeli setting: "The tendency to live inside a narrative of misery and suffering leads either to justification of unethical things or to the desire to simply flee."

I thought about the Israelis I've spoken with, the people I knew who justified things they would never have justified before the war, and the people I knew who had left. Victimhood was the engine of both.

"But I was also in places in Africa with enormous pride, a kind of self-confidence. I experienced this very strongly in some parts of Kenya. People are very, very proud of their story and their narrative. And when they arrive at that place – pride as opposed to victimhood – suddenly it's easier for them to hear criticism. And easier for them to hear other opinions. And to contain complexity. From a place of confidence."

This was the lesson Yau brought home from East Africa. The capacity to hold complexity is not based on intellectual acumen. It is not a product of education or sophistication or goodwill. It is a product of confidence. When you are secure in the basics – your right to exist, your dignity, your ability to defend yourself – you can hear things that challenge your narrative without feeling attacked. When you are not secure, every challenge feels existential, and you harden your heart. You cannot listen. You cannot hold two things at once. You can only defend. Security, on a narrative level, on a spiritual level, on an emotional level, enables complexity, enables accepting that others feel differently and acknowledging their right to do so. The story a people tells itself creates the reality they experience, either for good or for ill. If we can get the story right, the frame right, we might even be able to solve the physical challenges we face.

"My Promised Land is a Promised Land that is ultimately based on a great deal of self-confidence. The greater our self-confidence in the basic things – the right to exist, human dignity, all these things – the easier it is to contain these complexities. Easier to contain things that perhaps even contradict part of our narrative, because it won't threaten them."

When I asked him to be more specific and describe, practically, what that looks like to him, he referred to Theodor Herzl's *Altneuland* – the novel that imagined the Jewish state before it existed. Reading it changed how he thought about Israel and its history.

"I read it and said: wow, this sounds amazing. Why didn't we do this? A state deeply rooted in Judaism and in the right of existence of Jews and of Israel, on one hand. On the other hand, very pluralistic and accepting of differences. There's room for everyone, and everything runs as it should. A kind of return to this basis of existence is what I hope for."

At the same time, October 7th had taught him something about the limits of openness.

"October 7th was ultimately a kind of encounter with the wicked one. We experienced evil – it's not for nothing that people compare it to the Holocaust. It's like suddenly seeing that there is evil in the world that can do truly terrible things. So I need to learn how to deal, on one hand, with a pluralistic, open, accepting tendency – together with the fact that there is evil in the world. And I don't know exactly what that looks like."

He told me about a section of the Passover Haggadah that he particularly loves: the Four Sons. Four children, each coming from a different place, each asking a different question, even the wicked one. And all of them have a place at the table. The Haggadah does not expel the wicked son. It does not pretend he does not exist. It seats him beside the wise one and the simple one and the one who does not know how to ask, and it answers each of them on their own terms.

"The more we speak to the wicked ones from a place of confidence, the Promised Land will be more stable, stronger, and also better." The more we can access peace, too, as he defines it. "Peace as the default mode of thinking and working. Both internal peace among us. And also peace with the neighbors. And this is a peace that doesn't come through giving up who we are or self-negation. It comes from a place of enormous confidence. Confidence in who we are. In identity. And it's a quiet confidence – because it's confidence that allows different opinions and allows telling stories in different ways."

He told me about something his wife had described: how, on an Instagram group for mothers sharing birth stories, an Israeli woman shared her experience of giving birth during the war, not knowing if she'd have to run to a shelter mid-labor. The responses were all from people dismissing her: "but what about Gaza?" As if acknowledging one woman's difficulty meant negating another's suffering. As if there were a finite amount of compassion in the world, and every drop spent on an Israeli was a drop stolen from a Palestinian.

"I want us not to have that anymore. I want us to have the ability to recognize everyone's difficulty and everyone's narratives, without feeling threatened. But this path must go through feeling very, very secure in who we are."

"And ultimately this probably needs to be a return to the basics. A return to the values, both Jewish and universal, that this state was built on. Some kind of constitution, some kind of agreement that is very concrete. And through that we'll find it easier to develop this confidence, and then to open into this pluralistic state that I'm imagining."

What stays with me from my conversation with Yau is how he describes the infrastructure for hope, and bases it on a foundation of complexity. He is not a dreamer – he measures and evaluates for a living, he works in broken societies, he knows what victimhood does to people and what confidence makes possible. He has a father who lives in a settlement and holds anti-apartheid convictions and complex opinions that do not fit into any box. He has a wife who discovered, with shock, what it means to be Israeli in the world. He has a Palestinian colleague who apologized on October 7th only to grieve for Gaza and his family's community in the West Bank in the months after. And from all of them he learned that complexity is not the enemy of identity. Its existence is proof of an identity's strength.

His daughter, Nova, was born one year before October 7th, in a world so very different from the one she will grow up in. When she is old enough he will tell her about the shattering, the mourning, the mobilization, the caring that makes Israelis different. He will tell her about the evil they encountered, and the war that lost its justification, and the government that refused to say what yes. And he will tell her that the people did not stop speaking, did not stop caring, did not stop doing. That even in a country run by leaders who said only what no, the people kept insisting on what yes.

I agree with Yau: I too believe that what will kill Israel is not wars. It is the loss of hope. It is its abandonment by good people who have given up. It is the simplification of a complex reality that reflects the legitimate aspirations of human beings who want to self-determine and deserve the right to do so. And above all else I agree with him that the work required of our leaders now, of all of us now, is to restore the vision of what yes. What we are building. What we want. What the Promised Land actually looks like, imagined it from a place of confidence rather than fear.

Aliza Inbal

There is no place in the world that Aliza Inbal would rather be than in Jerusalem.

She knows this because she has taken the time to explore the alternatives and knows with certainty where she is meant to be. She has lived elsewhere. She grew up in Canada, moved to Israel, lived in DC, Brussels, Kinshasa, London. She worked for the World Bank, traveled to Ukraine, Rwanda, the DRC. She has seen the world. She came back to Jerusalem. She will stay.

"I love the fact that Jerusalem is so multicultural. And by multicultural I mean Arabs and Christians and Haredim – ultra-Orthodox. I love that. I think that it should enhance life for everybody here. The fact that it doesn't at the moment is not because it shouldn't, and that it can't, and hopefully one day it will."

That last clause, hopefully one day, is the hook on which everything else she believes hangs. It defines her: a specific hope about what she can't see around the corner but knows is there, or is coming. A potential embedded in the present. A future that is awaiting to be revealed.

To understand her commitment, it helps to first understand how she defines Zionism. Because her Zionism is the mirror image of the neo-Zionism, the militant Judeanism practiced ostentatiously by the Israeli right, which she hates for its supremacy, for its rejection of the multiculturalism on display in the city she loves. Her Zionism is the one that created the State, created the conditions for Jerusalem's kaleidoscopic beauty, and has given her the opportunity to be herself, as Jew, alongside others who share equal love for the land and its history.

"Zionism is only that the Jews have a right to live, and have full civil and political rights, in their historic homeland. That's it. And for me, that doesn't mean to the exclusion of anyone. Because I think that the Palestinians have a right to live in their historic homeland as well. I don't see one claim trumping the other."

This is the Zionism I hold as well. Not a license for dominance. Not as the sole claim to the right of self-determination. A claim to the right to determine one's own destiny, to being the hero of one's own historic story. To authentically make that claim, one must also extend that same claim to others. This is the Zionist that was envisioned by the founders of the movement, reflected in their books and essays and speeches, shared by the different ideological streams of the movement and enshrined in Israel's Declaration of Independence.

There is also a personal dimension to this that precedes politics, for Aliza. She was born in Canada. Her father was born in Canada, his parents were born in Poland. But her mother was born in Israel. Her grandparents grew up in Israel, what was then called the British Mandate of Palestine. Like mine, they were Palestinian citizens.

"We don't have another place that is ours. And if I can be accepted as a Canadian for having been there for one generation, why can't I be accepted as belonging to this place when there are a lot of generations behind me?"

She says this not to mount a legal argument to justify her presence but to describe something she feels, the kind of truth that does not require external validation because it simply is true. And when people frame Israel as uniquely colonial, she finds it not just wrong but a blatant falsehood.

"The majority of Israelis are actually indigenous to this region. Two-thirds of the population from 1948 until the Russians came in the early 1990s were people from the Middle East, most of whom were kicked out of other Arab countries." Refugees who went to the only country that would take them in. Having lived in other countries as a humanitarian aid worker, she does not understand how people could make the case that some people have the right to be legitimate immigrants and leave countries of persecution to find a better life, while the Jews are not. Which is why the question she now wrestles with, when it comes to Israel, is not whether she has a right to be here – obviously, objectively, she does – but what being here requires of her.

For a long time, nearly two decades, she avoided answering that question.

Years ago, Aliza had been deeply involved in the Oslo process as a young staffer in the Israeli Foreign Ministry, organizing people-to-people events across Jordan, Egypt, and the Palestinian territories. Writing speeches for then-prime minister Yitzhak Rabin. She felt fortunate to work to realize her ideals and build a better future for her people. Until it crashed all around her.

"I was very, very, very involved in Oslo. And when it fell apart with the second intifada – which for me was when I fell apart – I remember thinking to myself clearly: the time isn't right to solve the Arab-Israeli conflict. We're not going to be able to progress towards a two-state solution at the moment."

So she left the Foreign Ministry in 2004, and decided to devote herself to tackling a different problem with what she felt at the time had greater chances of success: "I can't solve or be part of a solution to the Arab-Israeli conflict right now. So why didn't I solve something easy, like global poverty?"

She studied towards her doctorate. She went to work for the World Bank. She built an NGO oriented around making Israel a force of good in the world. She allowed herself not to think about what was happening between Israel and the Palestinians in the land between the river and the sea.

"For twenty years, from 2004 till October 7, 2023, I just forgot that there was an Israeli-Arab conflict. I was off doing good and doing things that I felt were positive in the world. And I just ignored what was going on in the territories as if – because we weren't dealing with it – it went away."

It was during those twenty years that I met her. I vividly remember a ride I caught with her from Tel Aviv to a conference called ID2: Israeli Designed International Development, organized by Daniel Ben Yehuda and Danielle Abraham, and sponsored by the Schusterman Family Foundation. The year was 2014, and the conference was held up the coast from Tel Aviv, in Caesarea in February, a beautiful time of year where the often yellowed and browned slopes of the Carmel mountain range turned green and were covered in multicolored blankets of flowers. We were both invited to speak there, she about her work, me about the work MobileODT was doing to transform cervical cancer screening in emerging markets.

As we drove we spoke about our past as activists, our hopes for the future of this region. Spoke about how, despite the intermittent wars between Israel and Gaza – the last one was two years earlier, the next one would be months away from that moment in 2014 – we felt that the future was getting brighter. That both Jews and Arabs were realizing that there was more to live for than to die for, that the conflict might actually be paved over by the road to normalcy.

I remembering looking out as we passed the Havatzelet Junction and the old, run-down youth village planted there, and telling her my vision for the university I would love to build there: a new sort of learning environment for people of the region, an applied research and development center bringing together our neighbors to collaborate on solving the largest problems facing the Levant. Telling her that I would make it happen if not in ten years, in twenty.

Less than a decade later, those dreams were fractured.

On October 7th, Aliza's friends were killed by the Gazan gangs led by Hamas into Israel's south. Her close colleagues were kidnapped. Aliza knew more people in Kibbutz Be'eri than in any other kibbutz in Israel. In the early weeks she helped resettle families displaced from the South, doing what was needed. She was in shock just like everyone else she knew.

But she also had a friend from Gaza. A colleague from the Oslo years, now in London, whose entire family remained in Gaza.

"Someone once said about the hostages that we all have our own hostage. We may not know any hostages, but when we think about the hostages, each of us has a face we think about. His family were my Gazans. And every single day I thought about his family."

"October 7th was an enormous wake-up call. I suddenly realized that just because I've been ignoring the occupation didn't mean it didn't exist."

In the midst of her mourning, the midst of recounting the vast tragedies that were levied on the people she loved, she emphasized that she believed that Israel shared responsibility for setting the scene for October 7th. For decades we lived as if the status quo would just work itself out: Israel would rule over Palestinians militarily, and the Palestinians would just accept their lot in life. Our government, on the other hand, led by

Benjamin Netanyahu, went further: to maintain this status quo, to undercut the Palestinian Authority and its quest for statehood, the government decided to strengthen Hamas as a counterweight to national independence. They explicitly told Israelis that Hamas was an asset, a tool to ensure Israel's perpetual control of the land between the river and the sea.

So while the occupation did not justify the horrific violence – because nothing can justify the choice of human beings with mothers and sisters and fathers and brothers to rape and mutilate and kill other human beings – the way Netanyahu's successive governments used Hamas as a tool certainly set the stage for violence against Israelis. And we, who had ignored the issue, who had imagined that Israel could devote itself to international development and bettering the world without first addressing the injustices in our near abroad, had a part in that.

It was in the midst of this storm of emotions – grief for Israeli friends killed, grief for a Gazan's friend's family, the recognition that both were just as precious, just as human – that she reached for Albert O. Hirschman and what she learned from him in order to explain to me why she remained committed to Israel. To Zionism.

Hirschman was born at the turn of the twentieth century as a German Jew. He studied economics. He went to fight in the Spanish Civil War against the fascists. He returned to Germany, fled the Nazis, and made his way to France, where he joined the effort to smuggle refugees. Not the famous Jews the

International Rescue Committee prioritized, but ordinary ones, across the Pyrenees into Spain and Portugal and freedom.

"He knew how to do it because he had fought in the Spanish Civil War," she said. "He did this for a while."

He eventually made it to America, became a professor, and developed a theory she is certain must have come from his own experience of loss and commitment. The question he set out to answer was: what do you do when something you love changes into something you cannot accept?

"He says: when you have a brand that you love – be it classic Coke or Zionism – and that brand changes, you have three choices."

The first is exit. You stop believing. You leave.

The second is loyalty. You believe in the brand, so you believe the change must be right. Whatever the leadership is doing must be good, because the brand is good.

"The last one is voice. And voice is saying: I love this too much to let go."

"I could not be loyal to what this government was doing. Which left me with two choices: exiting – saying it's not my brand anymore – or voice. Trying to change that vision of Zionism to the vision of Zionism that I hold. And so that's where I stand now."

I asked her: why not exit?

"Because this country is my family. It's like – you don't leave your family, or you don't kick your kids out of the house, just because they start behaving in ways that are unconscionable."

In the early days of the war, she found herself in conversations about leaving, the kind Israelis have in extremity, testing the thought. She noticed something: "There is no place in the world that I would rather be than in Jerusalem. And I remember understanding how heartbreaking it must be to be a refugee, because I knew how heartbreaking it would be for me not to live here."

The other reason is ethical: "Ever since October 7th, all I think about is ethics. I think about ethics like men are supposed to think about the Roman Empire. I just think about ethics all of the time."

Staying, for her, is the more ethical choice. Not the easier one.

"If I leave, I'm not helping my friend's family in Gaza and I'm not helping Palestinians who are beset by settler violence. The only way I can help is by being here. And I do feel I have a moral obligation to, if not right the wrongs, at least combat the wrongs that my government is doing in my name."

She has a colleague at UNICEF, a European, not Jewish, who has served in the Middle East and has a Levantine girlfriend. Since the beginning of the war, he writes to her regularly to criticize Israel, to eviscerate it. It is always him who initiates.

Shortly after October 7th, she responded to his message saying he hoped no one she knew was hurt with a list: friends who were kidnapped, colleagues whose children had been killed. He did not respond immediately. Then, about a week into the war, he wrote back to say he was disgusted by what Hamas had done to Israel, and equally disgusted by what Israel was doing in Gaza. And then he would write again, only focused on Israel, only to tell her how wrong her country was.

"Every so often he reaches out to me to send me another atrocity. And I keep saying to him: why? Like, what do you want me to say?"

She was not asking him rhetorically. She genuinely wants to understand why this conflict, of all conflicts, commands his attention so completely. He, on the other hand, ignores her questions, only to write another blistering accusation.

"I know why I'm fixated on this issue. It is my responsibility to speak up and do everything I can to stop this violence. It is a little worrisome that other people are fixated on us to the extent that they can't see human misery elsewhere."

And she is, indeed, fixated. She hates her government. She has gone out to the streets every Saturday night of the past three years to protest, though she is not sure it helps. She believes the military response to the Hamas-led attacks was, at its outset, inevitable – like most Israelis, she understood there had to be some response. That the fundamental responsibility of the state is to protect its citizens, and sometimes that means using necessary force to defend its citizens from threat. And she believes, like many Israelis, that at some point the government crossed the line between legitimate response and cruelty and callousness.

"What was the day that I said this has gone too far? I don't know. I can't pinpoint that exact day. But it did happen." The turning point, for her, was when the government started getting involved with aid. "Starving people to death is definitely an incorrect application of power. And I don't think it enhances our security. I think it reduces our security."

Yet despite the depths of the destruction and deprivation, the mounting casualties, she remained committed to using her voice. To do what she could to raise awareness and to support efforts to hold the government accountable. Because she does believe there have been humanitarian atrocities. That the war has been one of immense destruction. That the destruction may have started off with legitimate aims, but was forced by politics to go to lengths that are no longer legitimate. "A lot of what this war has been for me is thinking: we would never do anything like that. And then it turning out that we did do something like that."

The key word here is 'we.' Because Aliza does not distance herself from responsibility by attributing it entirely to the government she opposes. She is Israeli. The army acts in her name. The moral weight lands on her whether she accepts it or not, and she accepts it because she recognizes her commitment to Zionism as an obligation to the State's future.

One way she acts on that responsibility is by driving to the West Bank twice a week.

There is a group of Bedouin families living along the road to the Dead Sea, extended families, each in their own area, living in structures that barely qualify as shelter, whose water pipes settlers cut, whose land Jewish extremists are gradually taking away from them by force. She goes to sit with them, the Bedouin. Not because she believes her single visit will change the situation, but because the Jewish extremists behave differently when Israeli Jews are watching. And she has noticed something strange happen to her sense of self on that road.

"One of the really weird things that happens when you are there all the time: when you see a car coming towards you on the very narrow, winding dirt road, the first thing you think is: is it one of us or is it one of them? But our definitions of us and them have changed. Because if I see a yellow license plate, I think: it's one of them. And if I see a green license plate, I think: it's one of us."

Israeli plates are yellow. Palestinian plates are green.

"I feel like – okay, that's fine. Which is so bizarre. And it really isn't because I feel less Israeli. It's because these violent settlers are not my people."

So I asked her the first question that came to my mind in response: who are your people? And what sort of political solution would you propose?

She answered me first with a joke: "Two states. One for all of the people that believe we should have two states, whether they're Jewish or Arab, and one for all of the people who believe there's only room for one nation between the river and the sea."

She paused. Then: "Unfortunately, that would mean I couldn't stay in Jerusalem. Which is why I've switched over to the binational state solution."

Aliza believes the Zionist thing to do, the right thing to do, would be to work towards what she might call a Canadian solution, a binational state where twenty percent of the population is French-speaking and the mechanisms of the state are built to reflect that, imperfectly but authentically. The French Canadians had once been a disadvantaged, discriminated-against population. They built political power. The state changed with them, although it is far from perfect. Some Quebecois still threaten to leave, still protest that the country they live in is too biased towards its English-Canadian identity. But most Canadians themselves are proud of their multicultural identity and the functionally binational reality of Canada, as imperfect as it might be. Israel could be structured similarly, in her opinion, with Arabic speakers as opposed to French speakers.

Her dream reflects what she loves about her city: multicultural, multilingual, imperfect, and worth staying in. So too, she believes, could be Israel. Just because her dream remains deferred does not mean she believes it will never come true. Nor does it mean she believes there is any justice in calls for Israel's dissolution, or for Jews to abandon the Zionist project.

Aliza is not alone in imagining a future for Israel that is both proudly a Jewish homeland, a State for the Jews, and deeply multicultural. In 2023, before October 7, the idea of Federalizing Israel grew in prominence due to a growing recognition that even amongst Israel's Jews there were multiple visions for how Jewish the State of Israel could and should be. Some advocated a split along historical lines, a religious Judea in the hills, and a secular Israel along the coasts. Others advocated for a Swiss Canton system, with leadership shared among the statelets that would make up a federated Israel. The former head of Israel's National Economic Council, and the economic advisor to Prime Minister Netanyahu from 2009-2015, Eugene Kandel, proposed a system he called *Alumot* to allow for communal membership decoupled from geographic restrictions.

I personally have been a fan of a twelve state solution, ever since I learned of the idea proposed by Judd Yadid in 2012. This vision, inspired by the tribal confederation that represents the Children of Israel's longest historic period of autonomy, would be defined by regional entities, each with a distinct identity and able to nurture their chosen way of life, reflecting the differing lifestyles of the rainbow of peoples who make up modern Israel. They would share a common infrastructure for defense, finance, and health, and regionalize everything else.

But whether it be a Canadian solution, a three state solution, a five state solution, a seven state federation, or a twelve state confederation, the point Aliza made remains the same: the State of Israel we are experiencing today is not the State of Israel we must accept for evermore. States change. Nations evolve. They respond to the realities of the world and the collective will of their people, whether through the ballot box or through popular pressure. And if enough of us are willing to devote even a bit of our lives, a bit of our energies, to transforming Israel for the better, I believe we can make it so.

"The mindset I have is: I'm the Free French. It's a long battle. The battle for an enlightened Israel, whatever Israel may look like in the future, is not something that's going to be won in a year or two years. But we have to fight the fight."

The Free French fought because they loved their country. They fought without certainty, without a visible end in sight, against powers that seemed insurmountable. They fought because stopping was not an option. Aliza is not claiming equivalence between the Free French and the Israeli-flag waving liberal democrats protesting today. The government of Israel is not populated by Nazi sympathizers, even if they are extremists. They are not fascists, even if some of their rhetoric borders on fascistic. They are not bent on exterminating Palestinians, despite ordering a brutal war, even if some members of the government would not bat an eye at the ethnic cleansing of Gaza. Unlike the Free French, she is not advocating armed insurrection. She is borrowing a posture, the commitment of people who could not see the end of the war but kept fighting the battles to build the state they could live in, imperfect as it would become.

The organization Aliza has placed her faith in is Standing Together, a grassroots movement of Jewish and Arab citizens of Israel. What she loves about it is not what it opposes. It is what it affirms.

"Their vision is a vision of love and not of hate. It isn't a vision which says it's bad for Jews to be here, that Jews should not be allowed to be here, or Arabs should not be allowed to be here. It's a vision that says: we are all citizens of this country and we have to find a way to forge a shared future. And we can find a way to forge a shared future."

I agree. Herzl envisioned an Israel where Arabs were equal citizens and equally invested in the success of the Zionist entity. So did Jabotinsky. Jews in the United States are more often than not proud Americans, despite America's clear Christian heritage, just as they are in England, a country led by a monarch who is also the head of the national church. Israeli identity has already functionally expanded to include non-Jews within it. Arab and Palestinian Israelis have been a critical backbone for the country for years, in healthcare, in education, in the public service. There is no reason why we cannot forge a national identity backed up by a national narrative that embraces non-Jewish Israelis as Israelis, through and through. Ensures their place at the heart of our Hebrew Republic.

"Even the Hundred Years' War ended after a Hundred years."

Aliza does not know when this war will end. But she has a vision for what winning looks like, and she is committed to staying and fighting and has chosen the only option that makes sense to her: Voice.

Conclusion

Every once in a while I think back to a conversation I had with Frances Miriam Kreimer at Columbia, in the Fall of 2004, about Israel, about Zionism, about her rejection of the concept of choseness, and about the imagery of Israel as a light unto the nations. We were reading the political philosopher Michael Walzer's *Exodus and Revolution* on the morality embedded in the story of Israel's auto-emancipation from Egypt and, perhaps inspired by it, I remember making the following argument for the first time: just because we aspire to be a light unto the nations does not mean other nations do not have their own light to shine. It also does not deny that darkness may overwhelm if we do not nurture that light.

I think about that imagery often, every time someone says that Zionism is supremacist, that violence in Zionism is a feature not a bug, or, alternatively, when I hear that Zionism necessitates a rejection of Palestinian self-determination, or that supporting Israel means opposing Palestine.

The thing about light is that it only adds to other lights. It never takes away. Same with love. Love – the foundation of choseness – is a renewable resource. One chooses to love one person one way and another in another. Just because I love my wife does not mean I do not love my friends. My life is richer because I am able to love different people differently, to choose different people for different relationships.

This understanding has only deepened as I became a parent thrice over. As a father, I tell each of my children that I love them the most in the entire world. That they are my favorite. And I say so in front of their brother, their sister, and they know that they each are my favorite, that I love each of them more than they will ever know.

Loving a child, loving a sibling, loving a parent, and for some of us loving a life partner, is not always easy. Things break. Mistakes are made. Sometimes terrible mistakes, sometimes mistakes that keep us up at night and shame us. Love – true love, not romantic love, love as in *Ahava* which is the bedrock of covenant and commitment – is the beginning of the cure for such mistakes. The basis to rebuild and rehabilitate.

I have come to believe that Israel's destruction of Gaza was an immoral act, a political act, a callous and terrible act that harmed far too many innocents. That it came after the terrible violence of October 7th, 2023, was doubly tragic: the unforgivable attacks planned and executed by the government of Gaza on Israeli civilians caused physical and emotional harm to Israel that is hard enough to overcome. Adding the moral injury of the destruction of Gaza to the terrible memory of that day, adding the guilt and the shame to Israelis who saw the worst of their human nature on display, will, I believe, be similarly unforgettable.

I know I am not alone in feeling this, and I know there are many Israelis who would strenuously disagree with me. Their arguments have not changed my position. I believe Israel could have fought this war differently.

I believe Israel's war on Gaza was, at its beginning, a just war, a war imposed on it by a terrible group of religious extremists who intended to genocide the Jews. I feel ashamed that Israel's government, my government, decided to pursue the course of action that it did, and did not have the wisdom and foresight to recognize that there were better ways to defend our people and build a better future for us and our region.

But in the absence of that sort of leadership, we Israelis who see both the bad and the good and the destruction and the potential peeking through the cracks need to be the leaders Israel needs. We need allies, too: Jews and non-Jews who care about Israel, who believe in the collective potential of the Jewish People to contribute towards fixing the world in our unique way. We need those who can help us nurture our particular light unto the nations, who can help protect it from being snuffed out, and who can reflect that light back amongst the other lights of the nations who share our commitment to building a better world.

The story of the Children of Israel, the story of the Tribe of Abraham, is a long and difficult one. From its first moments there was rivalry and disquiet, jealousy and intrigue. There was also love. Love between Abraham and Hagar, love between Ishmael and Itzhak. Love eventually replaced hate between

Jacob and Esau, between Joseph and his brothers, when each assumed responsibility for their actions. A love based on accountability and a commitment to mutual wellbeing that healed past violence and betrayal.

When Peter Beinart, when Avrum Burg, when anti-Zionist (and some antizionist) Jews speak about the destruction of Gaza as either the proof that we Jews do not deserve to govern ourselves, or that we Israelis have led to the destruction of Jewish civilization, when they then go on to advocate for the state's dissolution, I believe they have objectified Israelis, minimized us and our love for Israel. For each other. They've forgotten the dedication Israelis have proven to making an embodied and empowered Jewish community thrive. Their willingness to struggle against the odds to build a political community that reflects the best in them.

It is silly to entertain a theoretical debate as to whether the Jews should seek a state. Israel, factually, exists. Approximately half of the world's Jews call it their home and, through their political organizing, determine its actions. Israeli's commitment to the state is due to their commitment to their people. Due to their commitment to their Judaism. Their culture. Their morality. Their ethics. Their art. Their desire to live a life determined by their ideals expressed in their own words, in their own language, in a place that defined their people's history, and their willingness to fight, to march, to protest, to stand in solidarity, to mobilize in order to build a state that chooses life.

When anti-Zionists speak about Israel as an impediment or harm to Judaism, therefore, I think they've lost touch with what Judaism is: the organizing framework determining the communal life of the Jewish People. They've forgotten what being a Jew requires: solidarity with one's family, commitment to one's kin, a covenant with one's tribe. A fierce pride in being who we are, in not assimilating away. Proud of our uniqueness and dedicated to seeing it through to its collective expression. I think those willing to do away with Israel have romanticized the powerlessness of exile and forgotten the reasons for our exile. Forgotten that exile was not of our choosing then, and will not be of our choosing now. And I think they've invested themselves so deeply into the identity of the underdog that they've forgotten that every underdog either becomes the alpha or submits itself to the alpha's whims in return for protection.

All of this is to say that the Jews are a special and unique people, just as special and unique as every other people, cast in the image of the Creator like all other humans, able to use power for good as well as for evil. We deserve no less, and no more, than any other people, because every people should aspire to become a light unto the nations. We are no less worthy of being chosen, of choosing ourselves. Israel is the infrastructure for our collective expression. Or as Mordechai Kaplan beautifully described it, an instrument upon which the Jewish People may play their unique tune for humanity.

Even though we may agree that Israel has made mistakes, terrible mistakes, tragic mistakes, I believe those mistakes do not justify calls to deny millions of people the right to self-determination.

Those Jews living at home or abroad who feel uncomfortable with the decisions made by Netanyahu's successive governments should join Israelis in the struggle to prevent them from happening again. They can do so by supporting the organizations mentioned in this book, or by helping to create others. They can do so by cultivating complexity, recognizing that more than one thing can be true, more than one cause just. They can do so by envisioning Israel as they would want it to be and choosing to invest their energies into building a state they would be proud to call home.

Most of all, I believe they should do so by joining in the passionate, rowdy, contentious, generative workshop that is the modern State of Israel, the powerful yet imperfect instrument of the Jewish People.

Acknowledgments

This book exists because people were willing to sit with me and speak with honesty about things that are painful to discuss. Meredith Mishkin Rothbart, Danny Gordis, Alina Shkolnikov, David Green, Noa Keinan, Mike Berman, Michal Sherez Shilor, Bernie Avishai, Naama Klar, Yau Levy, and Aliza Inbal — I am grateful beyond what I can express here for your trust, your candor, and your time.

It would not have been possible without the support and encouragement of my wife, Erin Kopelow, who read early drafts and spurred me on; my brother, Tal Beery, who helped me craft its final approach; Shany Mor, who read and commented and challenged my approach; and Tomi Nelkin-Fantini who designed the cover. And my children who constantly inspire me to redouble my efforts to make Israel a place they – and their great grandparents – would be proud of.

A Note on the Organizations

Throughout this book, several organizations are mentioned whose work embodies the approach to Israel's present and future that its subjects describe. For readers who wish to learn more or support this work, brief descriptions follow.

Amal-Tikva: A Jewish-Arab peacebuilding organization co-founded by Meredith Mishkin Rothbart and Basheer Abu Baker. Its name means "hope" in both Arabic and Hebrew. Amal-Tikva trains peacebuilders, facilitates sustained Jewish-Palestinian dialogue, and channels funding to civil society organizations working on coexistence across the region. Learn more at: amal-tikva.org

Standing Together: A grassroots movement of Jewish and Arab citizens of Israel that organizes across ethnic and religious lines around shared economic and social concerns. Standing Together has been a leading voice for a negotiated end to the war and for equality within Israeli society. Learn more at: standing-together.org/en

The Tzedek Centers (Social Justice Centers): A network of grassroots social justice centers working at the intersection of Jewish and Arab communities across Israel. Michal Sherez

Shilor directs the Mixed Cities Department. Learn more at: merkazim.org

Hashomer Hatzair: The first Zionist youth movement, founded in a merger between Hashomer and Tzeiri Zion in 1913. For over a century, Hashomer Hatzair has led the fight for self-determination, social equality, and self-realization through collective mobilization. It has activities and camps across the world, including Camp Shomria in Liberty, New York where the author and his children grew up. Learn more at: campshomria.com

ANU: The Museum of the Jewish People, located at Tel Aviv University, is the world's leading institution dedicated to the story of the Jewish people across time and geography. Naama Klar heads the Koret School for Jewish Peoplehood there. Learn more at: anumuseum.org.il

Seeds of Peace: An international peacebuilding organization that brings together young people from conflict regions, including Israelis and Palestinians. Learn more at: www.seedsofpeace.org

Maoz: An organization focused on developing leadership for Israeli civil society. Learn more at: maoz-il.org/en

PresenTense: The movement for creative zionism which built an accelerator network for mission-driven social innovation in Israel and Jewish communities worldwide, co-founded by the author and Aharon Horwitz. Merged into Upstart in the US, and Appleseeds in Israel.

Rural Senses: A development analytics company founded by Yau Levy that helps international agencies understand and respond to the needs of people in the Global South. Learn more at ruralsenses.com

About the Author

Ariel Beery is a mission-driven entrepreneur and civil society activist who has spent three decades building institutions at the intersection of Israel, the Jewish world, and global development. He is the editor and publisher of Prophecy: A Journal for Tomorrow, and father of three.

Born in New York City and a long-time resident of Israel, he co-founded PresenTense, an operating platform for mission-driven innovation in Israel and Jewish communities worldwide, MobileODT, a medical technology company that transformed cervical cancer screening in emerging markets, and CoVelocity, an innovation workshop and advisory firm for organizations working towards the public good. He advises foundations, governments, and civil society organizations across Israel, Africa, and North America.

Being Israeli After the Destruction of Gaza is his second book, the first being a near-future science fiction published in 2012 on what could happen if a major social media company decided to take over the world. As if that could ever happen.

www.ingramcontent.com/pod-product-compliance
Lightning Source LLC
LaVergne TN
LVHW010657110826
845149LV00014B/3138